"[...] Gilbert's love of creativity is infectious, and there's a lot of great advice in this sunny book."

—*The Washington Post*

"[Gilbert] shares intimate glimpses into the life of a world-famous creative, complete with bouts of paralyzing fear and frustration, in an attempt to coax the rest of us into walking through the world just a little bit braver." —*Elle*

"Whatever your artistic pursuit, you'll nod in agreement as Elizabeth Gilbert reflects on the elusive, frustrating, and sometimes comically strange process of creativity. Thoughtful and funny, Gilbert makes an excellent case for doing whatever it takes to unlock your inner artist and find more joy in life." —*Woman's Day*

"Reading [*Big Magic*] is a little like having a coach by your side, cheering on your efforts—whatever they are—candidly and selflessly."

—*The Christian Science Monitor*

"Gilbert [writes] with sincerity and humility about the joy that creativity has given her. . . . If you enjoyed *Eat Pray Love,* if you are drawn to self-help or inspirational books, or if you just like to bask in another person's positive glow, you'll love *Big Magic.*" —Minneapolis *Star Tribune*

"[*Big Magic*] constitutes good advice . . . [in a voice that's] charming, personable, self-aware, jokey, conversational . . . [and] that Gilbert does so well." —*The New York Times Book Review*

"The *Eat Pray Love* author demystifies the tricky business of creativity. We're all ears." —*Cosmopolitan*

"Transformative." —*FlavorWire*

"The latest from Gilbert is all about you—that's 268 pages of practical advice for tapping into your own creativity. . . . Consider her your own personal life coach." —*Marie Claire*

"Gilbert demystifies the creative process, examining the practices of great artists to shed light on finding inspiration in the every day." —*Harper's Bazaar*

"Full of chatty advice, pep talks, amusing and inspiring stories . . . Gilbert's idea of living creatively may incorporate touches of magic, but she's practical in the extreme." —*The Miami Herald*

"A book-length meditation on inspiration." —*Newsday*

"A joyful ride through the enigmatic jungle of creative existence . . . [*Big Magic*] is not just about the production of artistic works but about building a life that nurtures the creative being in all of us." —*CREATIV Magazine*

"A booster that will help you out of any rut." —*Kansas City Star*

"A lucid and luminous inquiry into the relationship between human beings and the mysteries of the creative experience . . . Wholly electrifying." —*Brain Pickings*

"Elizabeth Gilbert is my new spirit animal. . . . I have profoundly changed my approach to creating since I read this book." —*The Huffington Post*

"A must read for anyone hoping to live a creative life . . . I dare you not to be inspired to be brave, to be free, and to be curious." —PopSugar

"[Gilbert will] make you feel giddy about creation." —*Medium*

"*Big Magic* ripples with Gilbert's enthusiasm, choice metaphor, and humor." —*LitHub*

"A must-read for anyone on the creative spectrum, from those who don't think there is a creative bone in their body to those who make a living from their artistic expression." —*Yakima Herald-Republic*

"The writing here is so friendly and funny that Gilbert's perspective on creative living goes down like lemonade in summer." —*BookPage*

"Part pat-on-the-back, part slap-in-the-face, [*Big Magic* is] . . . a fresh and modern surprise that fans of her work will relish." —*Wichita Eagle*

"Distinctly refreshing." —TED Ideas blog

"Gilbert leads readers through breaking out of their own creative ruts, finding fulfillment, and facing fear while finding balance between our spiritual and pragmatic beings. . . . Yes, please." —*Bustle*

"For anyone who's ever struggled with feeling worthy to express themselves through art, or been discouraged by the absence of inspiration, I'm not being hyperbolic when I say this book might just change your life." —MindBodyGreen

"A conversational, intimate glimpse into Gilbert's process and philosophy, as personable as a confab over coffee . . . Essential reading for anyone who wants to live a larger life, filled with more ideas, more projects, and more fulfillment . . . *Big Magic* is powerful stuff." —Barnes & Noble blog

"A transformative nonfiction treatise on creativity . . . Vibrant and inspirational." —*About Town Magazine*

"In her signature conversational style, both sassy and serious, Gilbert invokes high- and low-brow cultural references and recommends we channel our inner trickster. . . . [Her] manifesto is a book to read through quickly, and then start again to discover any big magic you may have missed." —KMUW

"Gilbert will completely change the way you think about the creative process." —*Indie Next List*

"A rewarding, motivating, and delightful read." —*Success* magazine

"A magnificent guide to how to be creative . . . [and] a heartfelt gem . . . Gilbert is determined to guide you into the light. Go with her." —*Jersey Journal*

"*Big Magic* [is] . . . fearless of voice and heart-opening in authenticity; in short, a book worthy of its name." —*Literary Inklings*

"Gilbert mines her writer's career to provide unique, inspiring, and constructive insights on how to navigate the wild ride that is the creative life. . . . Her charming nuggets are wise, comforting, and ultimately encouraging." —About.com

"There's nothing hippie-dippy about Gilbert's raw, honest, and downright hilarious observations of her own creative plight. . . . This isn't a How-To guide for creative living; this is the story of how one woman simply figured things out for herself, and learned how to live in harmony with her own creative soul. All can find a kind of solemn peace and reassurance in her words." —*Everyday Ebook*

"An empathetic and inspiring guide to mustering the courage to live a creative life. . . Nearly anyone who picks up this self-help manual should finish it feeling inspired, even if only to dream of a life without limits." —*Publishers Weekly* (starred review)

"Gilbert serves as an enthusiastic coach for readers who want more out of life. Highly recommended." —*Library Journal* (starred review)

Big Magic

Also by Elizabeth Gilbert

Pilgrims

Stern Men

The Last American Man

Eat Pray Love

Committed: A Love Story

At Home on the Range, by Margaret Yardley Potter

The Signature of All Things

Big Magic

Creative Living Beyond Fear

ELIZABETH GILBERT

RIVERHEAD BOOKS
NEW YORK

RIVERHEAD BOOKS
An imprint of Penguin Random House LLC
375 Hudson Street
New York, New York 10014

The Library of Congress has catalogued the Riverhead hardcover edition as follows:

Gilbert, Elizabeth, date.
Big magic : creative living beyond fear / Elizabeth Gilbert.
p. cm.
ISBN 9781594634710
1. Creative ability. 2. Inspiration. 3. Magical thinking. 4. Confidence.
5. Courage. 6. Conduct of life. I. Title.
BF408.G464 2015 2015010717
153.3'5—dc23

First Riverhead hardcover edition: September 2015
First Riverhead trade paperback edition: September 2016
Riverhead premium mass-market edition ISBN: 9780735214170

Printed in the United States of America
5 7 9 10 8 6 4

BOOK DESIGN BY AMANDA DEWEY

This one's for you, Rayya

Q: What is creativity?

A: The relationship between a human being and the mysteries of inspiration.

Contents

Courage

Hidden Treasure

Once upon a time, there was a man named Jack Gilbert, who was not related to me—unfortunately for me.

Jack Gilbert was a great poet, but if you've never heard of him, don't worry about it. It's not your fault. He never much cared about being known. But I knew about him, and I loved him dearly from a respectful distance, so let me tell you about him.

Jack Gilbert was born in Pittsburgh in 1925 and grew up in the midst of that city's smoke, noise, and industry. He worked in factories and steel mills as a young man, but was called from an early age to write poetry. He answered the call without hesitation. He became a poet the way other men become monks: as a devotional practice, as an act of love, and as a lifelong commitment to the search for grace and transcendence. I think this is probably a very good way to become a poet. Or to become anything, really, that calls to your heart and brings you to life.

Jack could've been famous, but he wasn't into it. He had the talent and the charisma for fame, but he never had the interest. His first collection, published in 1962, won the prestigious Yale Younger Poets prize and was nominated for the Pulitzer. What's more, he won over audiences as well as critics, which is not an easy feat for a poet in the modern world. There was something about him that drew people in and kept them captivated. He was handsome, passionate, sexy, brilliant on stage. He was a magnet for women and an idol for men. He was photographed for *Vogue*, looking gorgeous and romantic. People were crazy about him. He could've been a rock star.

Instead, he disappeared. He didn't want to be distracted by too much commotion. Later in life he reported that he had found his fame boring—not because it was immoral or corrupting, but simply because it was exactly the same thing every day. He was looking for something richer, more textured, more varied. So he dropped out. He went to live in Europe and stayed there for twenty years. He lived for a while in Italy, a while in Denmark, but mostly he lived in a shepherd's hut on a mountaintop in Greece. There, he contemplated the eternal mysteries, watched the light change, and wrote his poems in private. He had his love stories, his obstacles, his victories. He was happy. He got by somehow, making a living here and there. He needed little. He allowed his name to be forgotten.

After two decades, Jack Gilbert resurfaced and published another collection of poems. Again, the literary world fell in love with him. Again, he could have been famous. Again, he disappeared—this time for a decade. This would be his pattern always: isolation, followed by the publication of something sublime, followed by more isolation. He was like a rare orchid, with blooms separated by many years. He never promoted himself in the least. (In one of the few interviews he ever gave, Gilbert was asked how he thought his detachment from the publishing world had affected his career. He laughed and said, "I suppose it's been fatal.")

The only reason I ever heard of Jack Gilbert was that, quite late in his life, he returned to America and—for motives I will never know—took a temporary teaching position in the creative writing department at the University of Tennessee, Knoxville. The following year, 2005, it happened that I took exactly the same job. (Around campus, they started jokingly calling the position "the Gilbert Chair.") I found Jack Gilbert's books in my office—the office that had once been his. It was almost like the room was still warm from his presence. I read his poems and was overcome by their grandeur, and by how much his writing reminded me of Whitman. ("We must risk delight," he wrote. "We must have the stubbornness to accept our gladness in the ruthless furnace of this world.")

He and I had the same surname, we'd held the same job, we had inhabited the same office, we had taught many of the same students, and now I was in love with his words; naturally enough, I became deeply curious about him. I asked around: Who was Jack Gilbert?

Students told me he was the most extraordinary man they'd ever encountered. He had seemed not quite of this world, they said. He seemed to live in a state of uninterrupted marvel, and he encouraged them to do the same. He didn't so much teach them *how* to write poetry, they said, but *why*: because of delight. Because of stubborn gladness. He told them that they must live their most creative lives as a means of fighting back against the ruthless furnace of this world.

Most of all, though, he asked his students to be brave. Without bravery, he instructed, they would never be able to realize the vaulting scope of their own capacities. Without bravery, they would never know the world as richly as it longs to be known. Without bravery, their lives would remain small—far smaller than they probably wanted their lives to be.

I never met Jack Gilbert myself, and now he is gone—he passed away in 2012. I probably could've made it a personal mission to seek him out and meet him while he was living, but I never really wanted to. (Experience has taught me to be careful of meeting my heroes in person; it can be terribly disappointing.) Anyway, I quite liked the way he lived inside my imagination as a massive and powerful presence, built out of his poems and the stories I'd heard about him. So I decided to know him only that way—through my imagination. And that's where he remains for me to this day: still alive inside me, completely internalized, almost as though I dreamed him up.

But I will never forget what the real Jack Gilbert told somebody else—an actual flesh-and-blood person, a shy University of Tennessee student. This young woman recounted to me that one afternoon, after his poetry class, Jack had taken her aside. He complimented her work, then asked what she wanted to do with her life. Hesitantly, she admitted that perhaps she wanted to be a writer.

He smiled at the girl with infinite compassion and asked, "Do you have the courage? Do you have the courage to bring forth this work? The treasures that are hidden inside you are hoping you will say *yes*."

Creative Living, Defined

So this, I believe, is the central question upon which all creative living hinges: *Do you have the courage to bring forth the treasures that are hidden within you?*

Look, I don't know what's hidden within you. I have no way of knowing such a thing. You yourself may barely know, although I suspect you've caught glimpses. I don't know your capacities, your aspirations, your longings, your secret talents. But surely something wonderful is sheltered inside you. I say this with all confidence, because I happen to believe we are all walking repositories of buried treasure. I believe this is one of the oldest and most generous tricks the universe plays on us human beings, both for its own amusement and for ours: The universe buries strange jewels deep within us all, and then stands back to see if we can find them.

The hunt to uncover those jewels—that's creative living.

The courage to go on that hunt in the first place—that's what separates a mundane existence from a more enchanted one.

The often surprising results of that hunt—that's what I call Big Magic.

An Amplified Existence

When I talk about "creative living" here, please understand that I am not necessarily talking about pursuing a life that is professionally or exclusively devoted to the arts. I'm not saying that you must become a poet who lives on a mountaintop in Greece, or that you must perform at Carnegie Hall, or that you must win the Palme d'Or at the Cannes Film Festival. (Though if you want to attempt any of these feats, by all means, *have at it.* I love watching people swing for the bleachers.) No, when I refer to "creative living," I am speaking more broadly. I'm talking about living a life that is driven more strongly by curiosity than by fear.

One of the coolest examples of creative living that I've seen in recent years, for instance, came from my friend Susan, who took up figure skating when she was forty years old. To be more precise, she actually already knew how to skate. She had competed in figure skating as a child and had always loved it, but she'd quit the sport during adolescence when it became clear she didn't have quite enough talent to be a champion. (Ah, lovely adolescence—when the "talented" are officially shunted off from the herd, thus putting the total burden of society's creative dreams on the thin shoulders of a few select souls, while condemning everyone else to live a more commonplace, inspiration-free existence! What a system . . .)

For the next quarter of a century, my friend Susan did not skate. Why bother, if you can't be the best? Then she turned forty. She was listless. She was restless. She felt drab and heavy. She did a little soul-searching, the way one does on the big birthdays. She asked herself when was the last time she'd felt truly light, joyous, and—yes—*creative* in her own skin. To her shock, she realized that it had been decades since she'd felt that way. In fact, the last time she'd experienced such feelings had been as a teenager, back when she was still figure skating. She was appalled to discover that she had denied herself this life-affirming pursuit for so long, and she was curious to see if she still loved it.

So she followed her curiosity. She bought a pair of skates, found a rink, hired a coach. She ignored the voice within her that told her she was being self-indulgent and preposterous to do this crazy thing. She tamped down her feelings of extreme self-consciousness at being the only middle-aged woman on the ice, with all those tiny, feathery nine-year-old girls.

She just did it.

Three mornings a week, Susan awoke before dawn and, in that groggy hour before her demanding day job began, she skated. And she skated and skated and skated. And yes, she loved it, as much as ever. She loved it even more than ever, perhaps, because now, as an adult, she finally had the perspective to appreciate the value of her own joy. Skating made her feel alive and ageless. She stopped feeling like she was nothing more than a consumer, nothing more than the sum of her daily obligations and duties. She was making something of herself, making something *with* herself.

It was a revolution. A literal revolution, as she spun to life again on the ice—revolution upon revolution upon revolution . . .

Please note that my friend did not quit her job, did not sell her home, did not sever all her relationships and move to Toronto to study seventy hours a week with an exacting Olympic-level skating coach. And no, this story does not end with her winning any championship medals. It doesn't have to. In fact, this story does not end at all, because Susan is *still* figure skating several mornings a week—simply because skating is still the best way for her to unfold a certain beauty and transcendence within her life that she cannot seem to access in any other manner. And she would like to spend as much time as possible in such a state of transcendence while she is still here on earth.

That's all.

That's what I call creative living.

And while the paths and outcomes of creative living will vary wildly from person to person, I can guarantee you this: A creative life is an amplified life. It's a bigger life, a happier life, an expanded life, and a hell of a lot more interesting life. Living in this manner—continually and stubbornly bringing forth the jewels that are hidden within you—*is* a fine art, in and of itself.

Because creative living is where Big Magic will always abide.

Scary, Scary, Scary

Let's talk about courage now.

If you already have the courage to bring forth the jewels that are hidden within you, terrific. You're probably already doing really interesting things with your life, and you don't need this book. Rock on.

But if you don't have the courage, let's try to get you

some. Because creative living is a path for the brave. We all know this. And we all know that when courage dies, creativity dies with it. We all know that fear is a desolate boneyard where our dreams go to desiccate in the hot sun. This is common knowledge; sometimes we just don't know what to do about it.

Let me list for you some of the many ways in which you might be afraid to live a more creative life:

You're afraid you have no talent.
You're afraid you'll be rejected or criticized or ridiculed or misunderstood or—worst of all—ignored.
You're afraid there's no market for your creativity, and therefore no point in pursuing it.
You're afraid somebody else already did it better.
You're afraid everybody *else already did it better.*
You're afraid somebody will steal your ideas, so it's safer to keep them hidden forever in the dark.
You're afraid you won't be taken seriously.
You're afraid your work isn't politically, emotionally, or artistically important enough to change anyone's life.
You're afraid your dreams are embarrassing.

You're afraid that someday you'll look back on your creative endeavors as having been a giant waste of time, effort, and money.

You're afraid you don't have the right kind of discipline.

You're afraid you don't have the right kind of work space, or financial freedom, or empty hours in which to focus on invention or exploration.

You're afraid you don't have the right kind of training or degree.

You're afraid you're too fat. (I don't know what this has to do with creativity, exactly, but experience has taught me that most of us are afraid we're too fat, so let's just put that on the anxiety list, for good measure.)

You're afraid of being exposed as a hack, or a fool, or a dilettante, or a narcissist.

You're afraid of upsetting your family with what you may reveal.

You're afraid of what your peers and coworkers will say if you express your personal truth aloud.

You're afraid of unleashing your innermost demons, and you really *don't want to encounter your innermost demons.*

You're afraid your best work is behind you.
You're afraid you never had any best work to begin with.
You're afraid you neglected your creativity for so long that now you can never get it back.
You're afraid you're too old to start.
You're afraid you're too young to start.
You're afraid because something went well in your life once, so obviously nothing can ever go well again.
You're afraid because nothing has ever gone well in your life, so why bother trying?
You're afraid of being a one-hit wonder.
You're afraid of being a no-hit wonder . . .

Listen, I don't have all day here, so I'm not going to keep listing fears. It's a bottomless list, anyhow, and a depressing one. I'll just wrap up my summary this way: SCARY, SCARY, SCARY.

Everything is so goddamn scary.

Defending Your Weakness

Please understand that the only reason I can speak so authoritatively about fear is that I know it so intimately. I know every inch of fear, from head to toe. I've been a frightened person my entire life. I was born terrified. I'm not exaggerating; you can ask anyone in my family, and they'll confirm that, yes, I was an exceptionally freaked-out child. My earliest memories are of fear, as are pretty much all the memories that come after my earliest memories.

Growing up, I was afraid not only of all the commonly recognized and legitimate childhood dangers (the dark, strangers, the deep end of the swimming pool), but I was also afraid of an extensive list of completely benign things (snow, perfectly nice babysitters, cars, playgrounds, stairs, *Sesame Street*, the telephone, board games, the grocery store, sharp blades of grass, any new situation whatsoever, anything that dared to move, etc., etc., etc.).

I was a sensitive and easily traumatized creature who would fall into fits of weeping at any disturbance in her force field. My father, exasperated, used to call me Pitiful

Pearl. We went to the Delaware shore one summer when I was eight years old, and the ocean upset me so much that I tried to get my parents to *stop all the people on the beach from going into the surf.* (I just would've felt a lot more comfortable if everyone had stayed safely on his or her own towel, quietly reading; was that too much to ask?) If I'd had my way, I would have spent that entire vacation—indeed, my entire childhood—indoors, snuggled on my mother's lap, in low light, preferably with a cool washcloth on my forehead.

This is a horrible thing to say, but here goes: I probably would've *loved* having one of those awful Munchausen-syndrome-by-proxy mothers, who could have colluded with me in pretending that I was eternally sick, weak, and dying. I would have totally cooperated with that kind of mother in creating a completely helpless child, given half the chance.

But I didn't get that kind of mother.

Not even close.

Instead, I got a mother who wasn't having it. She wasn't having a minute of my drama, which is probably the luckiest thing that ever happened to me. My mom grew up on a farm in Minnesota, the proud product of tough Scandinavian immigrants, and she was not about to raise a little candy-ass. Not on her watch. My mother had a plan for turning around my fear that was almost comic in its straightforwardness: At every turn, she made me do exactly what I dreaded most.

Scared of the ocean? Get in that ocean!

Afraid of the snow? Time to go shovel snow!

Can't answer the telephone? You are now officially in charge of answering the telephone in this house!

Hers was not a sophisticated strategy, but it was consistent. Trust me, I resisted her. I cried and sulked and deliberately failed. I refused to thrive. I lagged behind, limping and trembling. I would do almost anything to prove that I was emotionally and physically totally enfeebled.

To which my mom was, like, "No, you aren't."

I spent years pushing back against my mother's unshakable faith in my strength and abilities. Then one day, somewhere in adolescence, I finally realized that this was a really weird battle for me to be fighting. Defending my weakness? That's seriously the hill I wanted to die on?

As the saying goes: "Argue for your limitations and you get to keep them."

Why would I want to keep my limitations?

I didn't, as it turned out.

I don't want you keeping yours, either.

Fear Is Boring

Over the years, I've often wondered what finally made me stop playing the role of Pitiful Pearl, almost overnight. Surely there were many factors involved in that evolution (the tough-mom factor, the growing-up factor), but mostly I think it was just this: I finally realized that my fear was boring.

Mind you, my fear had always been boring to everybody else, but it wasn't until mid-adolescence that it became, at last, boring even to me. My fear became boring to me, I believe, for the same reason that fame became boring to Jack Gilbert: *because it was the same thing every day.*

Around the age of fifteen, I somehow figured out that my fear had no variety to it, no depth, no substance, no texture. I noticed that my fear never changed, never delighted, never offered a surprise twist or an unexpected ending. My fear was a song with only one note—only one word, actually—and that word was "STOP!" My fear never had anything more interesting or subtle to offer than that one emphatic word, repeated at full volume on an endless loop: "STOP, STOP, STOP, STOP!"

Which means that my fear always made predictably boring decisions, like a choose-your-own-ending book that always had the same ending: *nothingness.*

I also realized that my fear was boring because it was identical to everyone else's fear. I figured out that everyone's song of fear has exactly that same tedious lyric: "STOP, STOP, STOP, STOP!" True, the volume may vary from person to person, but the song itself never changes, because all of us humans were equipped with the same basic fear package when we were being knitted in our mothers' wombs. And not just humans: If you pass your hand over a petri dish containing a tadpole, the tadpole will flinch beneath your shadow. That tadpole cannot write poetry, and it cannot sing, and it will never know love or jealousy or triumph, and it has a brain the size of a punctuation mark, but it damn sure knows how to be afraid of the unknown.

Well, so do I.

So do we all. But there's nothing particularly compelling about that. Do you see what I mean? You don't get any special *credit*, is what I'm saying, for knowing how to be afraid of the unknown. Fear is a deeply ancient instinct, in other words, and an evolutionarily vital one . . . but it ain't especially smart.

For the entirety of my young and skittish life, I had fixated upon my fear as if it were the most interesting thing about me, when actually it was the most mundane. In fact, my fear was probably the only 100 percent mundane thing about me. I had creativity within me that was original; I had a personality within me that was original; I had dreams and perspectives and aspirations within me that were original. But my fear was not original in the least. My fear wasn't some kind of rare artisanal object; it was just a mass-produced item, available on the shelves of any generic box store.

And that's the thing I wanted to build my entire identity around?

The most boring instinct I possessed?

The panic reflex of my dumbest inner tadpole?

No.

The Fear You Need and the Fear You Don't Need

Now you probably think I'm going to tell you that you must become fearless in order to live a more creative life. But I'm not going to tell you that, because I don't happen to believe it's true. Creativity is a path for the brave, yes, but it is not a path for the *fearless*, and it's important to recognize the distinction.

Bravery means doing something scary.

Fearlessness means not even understanding what the word *scary* means.

If your goal in life is to become fearless, then I believe you're already on the wrong path, because the only truly fearless people I've ever met were straight-up sociopaths and a few exceptionally reckless three-year-olds—and those aren't good role models for anyone.

The truth is, you need your fear, for obvious reasons of basic survival. Evolution did well to install a fear reflex within you, because if you didn't have any fear, you would lead a short, crazy, stupid life. You would walk into traffic. You would drift off into the woods and be eaten by bears.

You would jump into giant waves off the coast of Hawaii, despite being a poor swimmer. You would marry a guy who said on the first date, "I don't necessarily believe people were designed by nature to be monogamous."

So, yes, you absolutely do need your fear, in order to protect you from actual dangers like the ones I've listed above.

But you do not need your fear in the realm of creative expression.

Seriously, you don't.

Just because you don't *need* your fear when it comes to creativity, of course, doesn't mean your fear won't show up. Trust me, your fear will always show up—especially when you're trying to be inventive or innovative. Your fear will always be triggered by your creativity, because creativity asks you to enter into realms of uncertain outcome, and fear *hates* uncertain outcome. Your fear—programmed by evolution to be hypervigilant and insanely overprotective—will always assume that any uncertain outcome is destined to end in a bloody, horrible death. Basically, your fear is like a mall cop who thinks he's a Navy SEAL: He hasn't slept in days, he's all hopped up on Red Bull, and he's liable to shoot at his own shadow in an absurd effort to keep everyone "safe."

This is all totally natural and human.

It's absolutely nothing to be ashamed of.

It is, however, something that very much needs to be dealt with.

The Road Trip

Here's how I've learned to deal with my fear: I made a decision a long time ago that if I want creativity in my life—and I do—then I will have to make space for fear, too.

Plenty of space.

I decided that I would need to build an expansive enough interior life that my fear and my creativity could peacefully coexist, since it appeared that they would always be together. In fact, it seems to me that my fear and my creativity are basically conjoined twins—as evidenced by the fact that creativity cannot take a single step forward without fear marching right alongside it. Fear and creativity shared a womb, they were born at the same time, and they still share some vital organs. This is why we have to be careful of how we handle our fear—because I've noticed that when people try to kill off their fear, they often end up inadvertently murdering their creativity in the process.

So I don't try to kill off my fear. I don't go to war against it. Instead, I make all that space for it. Heaps of space. Every single day. I'm making space for fear right this moment. I allow my fear to live and breathe and stretch out its legs comfortably. It seems to me that the less I fight my fear, the less it fights back. If I can relax, fear relaxes, too. In fact, I cordially invite fear to come along with me everywhere I go. I even have a welcoming speech prepared for fear, which I deliver right before embarking upon any new project or big adventure.

It goes something like this:

"Dearest Fear: Creativity and I are about to go on a road trip together. I understand you'll be joining us, because you always do. I acknowledge that you believe you have an important job to do in my life, and that you take your job seriously. Apparently your job is to induce complete panic whenever I'm about to do anything interesting—and, may I say, you are *superb* at your job. So by all means, keep doing your job, if you feel you must. But I will also be doing my job on this road trip, which is to work hard and stay focused. And Creativity will be doing its job, which is to remain stimulating and inspiring. There's plenty of room in this vehicle for all of us, so make yourself at home, but understand this: *Creativity and I are the only ones who will be making any decisions along the way.* I recognize and respect that you are part of this family, and so I will never exclude you from our activities, but still—your suggestions will never be followed. You're allowed to have a seat, and you're allowed to have a voice, but you are not allowed to have a vote. You're not allowed to touch the road maps; you're not allowed to suggest detours; you're not allowed to fiddle with the temperature. Dude, you're not even allowed to touch the *radio.* But above all else, my dear old familiar friend, you are absolutely forbidden to drive."

Then we head off together—me and creativity and fear—side by side by side forever, advancing once more into the terrifying but marvelous terrain of unknown outcome.

Why It's Worth It

It isn't always comfortable or easy—carrying your fear around with you on your great and ambitious road trip, I mean—but it's always worth it, because if you can't learn to travel comfortably alongside your fear, then you'll never be able to go anywhere interesting or do anything interesting.

And that would be a pity, because your life is short and rare and amazing and miraculous, and you want to do really interesting things and make really interesting things while you're still here. I know that's what you want for yourself, because that's what I want for myself, too.

It's what we all want.

And you have treasures hidden within you—extraordinary treasures—and so do I, and so does everyone around us. And bringing those treasures to light takes work and faith and focus and courage and hours of devotion, and the clock is ticking, and the world is spinning, and we simply do not have time anymore to think so small.

Enchantment

An Idea Arrives

Now that we're done talking about fear, we can finally talk about magic.

Let me begin by telling you the most magical thing that's ever happened to me.

It's about a book that I failed to write.

My tale begins in the early spring of 2006. I had recently published *Eat Pray Love*, and I was trying to figure out what to do with myself next, creatively speaking. My instincts told me it was time to return to my literary roots and write a work of fiction—something I hadn't done in years. In fact, I hadn't written a novel in so long, I feared I had forgotten how to do it at all. I feared that fiction had become a language I could no longer speak. But now I had an idea for a novel—an idea that excited me tremendously.

The idea was based on a story that my sweetheart, Felipe, had told me one night about something that had happened in Brazil, back when he was growing up there in the 1960s. Apparently, the Brazilian government got a notion to build a giant highway across the Amazon jungle. This was during an era of rampant development and modernization, and such a scheme must have seemed stupendously forward-thinking at the time. The Brazilians poured a fortune into this ambitious plan. The international development community poured in many more millions. A staggering portion of this money immediately disappeared into a black hole of corruption and disorganization, but eventually enough cash trickled into the right places that the highway project finally began. All was going well for a few months. Progress was made. A short section of the road was completed. The jungle was being conquered.

Then it started to rain.

It seems that none of the planners of this project had fully grasped the reality of what the rainy season means in the Amazon. The construction site was immediately inundated and rendered uninhabitable. The crew had no choice but to walk away, leaving behind all their equipment under several feet of water. And when they returned many months later, after the rains had subsided, they discovered to their horror that the jungle had basically devoured their highway project. Their efforts had been erased by nature, as if the laborers and the road had never existed at all. They couldn't even tell where they had been working. All their heavy equipment was missing, too. It had not been stolen; it had simply been *swallowed.* As Felipe told it, "Bulldozers with tires as tall as a man had been sucked into the earth and disappeared forever. It was all gone."

When he told me this story—especially the part about the jungle swallowing up the machines—chills ran up my arms. The hairs on the back of my neck stood up for an instant, and I felt a little sick, a little dizzy. I felt like I was falling in love, or had just heard alarming news, or was looking over a precipice at something beautiful and mesmerizing, but dangerous.

I'd experienced these symptoms before, so I knew immediately what was going on. Such an intense emotional and physiological reaction doesn't strike me often, but it happens enough (and is consistent enough with symptoms reported by people all over the world, all throughout history) that I believe I can confidently call it by its name: inspiration.

This is what it feels like when an idea comes to you.

How Ideas Work

I should explain at this point that I've spent my entire life in devotion to creativity, and along the way I've developed a set of beliefs about how it works—and how to work with it—that is entirely and unapologetically based upon magical thinking. And when I refer to magic here, I mean it literally. Like, in the Hogwarts sense. I am referring to the supernatural, the mystical, the inexplicable, the surreal, the divine, the transcendent, the otherworldly. Because the truth is, I believe that creativity is a force of enchantment—not entirely human in its origins.

I am aware this is not an especially modern or rational way of seeing things. It is decidedly unscientific. Just the other day, I heard a respected neurologist say in an interview, "The creative process may seem magical, but it is not magic."

With all due respect, I disagree.

I believe the creative process is both magical *and* magic.

Because here is what I choose to believe about how creativity functions:

I believe that our planet is inhabited not only by animals and plants and bacteria and viruses, but also by *ideas.* Ideas are a disembodied, energetic life-form. They are completely separate from us, but capable of interacting with us—albeit strangely. Ideas have no material body, but they do have consciousness, and they most certainly have will. Ideas are driven by a single impulse: to be made manifest. And the only way an idea can be made manifest in our world is through collaboration with a human partner. It is only through a human's efforts that an idea can be escorted out of the ether and into the realm of the actual.

Therefore, ideas spend eternity swirling around us, searching for available and willing human partners. (I'm talking about *all* ideas here—artistic, scientific, industrial, commercial, ethical, religious, political.) When an idea thinks it has found somebody—say, you—who might be able to bring it into the world, the idea will pay you a visit. It will try to get your attention. Mostly, you will not notice. This is likely because you're so consumed by your own dramas, anxieties, distractions, insecurities, and duties that you aren't receptive to inspiration. You might miss the signal because you're watching TV, or shopping, or brooding over how angry you are at somebody, or pondering your failures and mistakes, or just generally really busy. The idea will try to wave you down (perhaps for a few moments;

perhaps for a few months; perhaps even for a few years), but when it finally realizes that you're oblivious to its message, it will move on to someone else.

But sometimes—rarely, but magnificently—there comes a day when you're open and relaxed enough to actually receive something. Your defenses might slacken and your anxieties might ease, and then magic can slip through. The idea, sensing your openness, will start to do its work on you. It will send the universal physical and emotional signals of inspiration (the chills up the arms, the hair standing up on the back of the neck, the nervous stomach, the buzzy thoughts, that feeling of falling into love or obsession). The idea will organize coincidences and portents to tumble across your path, to keep your interest keen. You will start to notice all sorts of signs pointing you toward the idea. Everything you see and touch and do will remind you of the idea. The idea will wake you up in the middle of the night and distract you from your everyday routine. The idea will not leave you alone until it has your fullest attention.

And then, in a quiet moment, it will ask, "Do you want to work with me?"

At this point, you have two options for how to respond.

What Happens When You Say No

The simplest answer, of course, is just to say no.

Then you're off the hook. The idea will eventually go away and—congratulations!—you don't need to bother creating anything.

To be clear, this is not always a dishonorable choice. True, you might sometimes decline inspiration's invitation out of laziness, angst, insecurity, or petulance. But other times you might need to say no to an idea because it is truly not the right moment, or because you're already engaged in a different project, or because you're certain that this particular idea has accidentally knocked on the wrong door.

I have many times been approached by ideas that I know are not right for me, and I've politely said to them: "I'm honored by your visitation, but I'm not your girl. May I respectfully suggest that you call upon, say, Barbara Kingsolver?" (I always try to use my most gracious manners when sending an idea away; you don't want word getting around the universe that you're difficult to work with.) Whatever your response, though, do be sympathetic to the poor idea. Remember: All it wants is to be realized. It's trying its best. It seriously has to knock on every door it can.

So you might have to say no.

When you say no, nothing happens at all.

Mostly, people say no.

Most of their lives, most people just walk around, day after day, saying no, no, no, no, no.

Then again, someday you just might say yes.

What Happens When You Say Yes

If you do say yes to an idea, now it's showtime.

Now your job becomes both simple and difficult. You have officially entered into a contract with inspiration, and you must try to see it through, all the way to its impossible-to-predict outcome.

You may set the terms for this contract however you like. In contemporary Western civilization, the most common creative contract still seems to be one of suffering. This is the contract that says, *I shall destroy myself and everyone around me in an effort to bring forth my inspira-*

tion, and my martyrdom shall be the badge of my creative legitimacy.

If you choose to enter into a contract of creative suffering, you should try to identify yourself as much as possible with the stereotype of the Tormented Artist. You will find no shortage of role models. To honor their example, follow these fundamental rules: Drink as much as you possibly can; sabotage all your relationships; wrestle so vehemently against yourself that you come up bloodied every time; express constant dissatisfaction with your work; jealously compete against your peers; begrudge anybody else's victories; proclaim yourself cursed (not blessed) by your talents; attach your sense of self-worth to external rewards; be arrogant when you are successful and self-pitying when you fail; honor darkness above light; die young; blame creativity for having killed you.

Does it work, this method?

Yeah, sure. It works great. Till it kills you.

So you can do it this way if you really want to. (By all means, do not let me or anyone else ever take away your suffering, if you're committed to it!) But I'm not sure this route is especially productive, or that it will bring you or your loved ones enduring satisfaction and peace. I will concede that this method of creative living can be extremely glamorous, and it can make for an excellent biopic after you die, so if you prefer a short life of tragic glamour to a long life of rich satisfaction (and many do), *knock yourself out.*

However, I've always had the sense that the muse of the tormented artist—while the artist himself is throwing temper tantrums—is sitting quietly in a corner of the studio, buffing its fingernails, patiently waiting for the guy to calm down and sober up so everyone can get back to work.

Because in the end, it's all about the work, isn't it? Or shouldn't it be?

And maybe there's a different way to approach it?

May I suggest one?

A Different Way

A different way is to cooperate fully, humbly, and joyfully with inspiration.

This is how I believe most people approached creativity for most of history, before we decided to get all *La Bohème* about it. You can receive your ideas with respect and curiosity, not with drama or dread. You can clear out whatever obstacles are preventing you from living your most creative life, with the simple understanding that whatever is bad for you is probably also bad for your work. You can lay off the booze a bit in order to have a keener mind. You can nourish healthier relationships in order to keep yourself undistracted by self-invented emotional catastrophes. You can dare to be pleased sometimes with what you have created. (And if a project doesn't work out, you can always think of it as having been a worthwhile and constructive experiment.) You can resist the seductions of grandiosity, blame, and shame. You can support other people in their creative efforts, acknowledging the truth that there's plenty of room for everyone. You can measure your worth by your dedication to your path, not by your successes or failures. You can battle your demons (through therapy, recovery, prayer, or humility) instead of battling your gifts—in part by realizing that your demons were never the ones doing the work, anyhow. You can believe that you are neither a slave to inspiration nor its master, but something far more interesting—its partner—and that the two of you are working together toward something intriguing and worthwhile. You can live a long life, making and doing really cool things the entire time. You might earn a living with your pursuits or you might not, but you can recognize that this is not really the point. And at the end of your days, you can thank creativity for having blessed you with a charmed, interesting, passionate existence.

That's another way to do it.

Totally up to you.

An Idea Grows

Anyhow, back to my story of magic.

Thanks to Felipe's tale about the Amazon, I had been visited by a big idea: to wit, that I should write a novel about Brazil in the 1960s. Specifically, I felt inspired to write a novel about the efforts to build that ill-fated highway across the jungle.

This idea seemed epic and thrilling to me. It was also daunting—what the hell did I know about the Brazilian Amazon, or road construction in the 1960s?—but all the good ideas feel daunting at first, so I proceeded. I agreed to enter into a contract with the idea. We would work together. We shook hands on it, so to speak. I promised the idea that I would never fight against it and never abandon it, but would only cooperate with it to the utmost of my ability, until our work together was done.

I then did what you do when you get serious about a

project or a pursuit: I cleared space for it. I cleaned off my desk, literally and figuratively. I committed myself to several hours of research every morning. I made myself go to bed early so I could get up at dawn and be ready for work. I said no to alluring distractions and social invitations so I could focus on my job. I ordered books about Brazil and I placed calls to experts. I started studying Portuguese. I bought index cards—my preferred method of keeping track of notes—and I allowed myself to begin dreaming of this new world. And in that space, more ideas began to arrive, and the outlines of the story started to take shape.

I decided that the heroine of my novel would be a middle-aged American woman named Evelyn. It is the late 1960s—a time of great political and cultural upheaval—but Evelyn is living a quiet life, as she always has done, in central Minnesota. She's a spinster who has spent twenty-five years working capably as an executive secretary at a large Midwestern highway construction firm. During that entire time, Evelyn has been quietly and hopelessly in love with her married boss—a kind, hardworking man who never sees Evelyn as anything but an efficient assistant. The boss has a son—a shady fellow, with big ambitions. The son hears about this giant highway project going on down in Brazil and persuades his father to put in a bid. The son uses his charm and coercion to convince the father to throw the family's entire fortune behind this enterprise. Soon enough, the son heads down to Brazil with a great deal of money and wild dreams of glory. Quickly, both the son and the money vanish. Bereft, the father dispatches Evelyn, his most trusted ambassador, to go to the Amazon to try to recover the missing young man and the missing cash. Out of a sense of duty and love, Evelyn heads to Brazil—at which point her orderly and unremarkable life is overturned as she enters into a world of chaos, lies, and violence. Drama and epiphanies follow. Also, it's a love story.

I decided I would call the novel *Evelyn of the Amazon.*

I wrote a proposal for the book and sent it to my publishing company. They liked it and they bought it. Now I entered into a second contract with the idea—a formal contract this time, with notarized signatures and deadlines and everything. Now I was fully invested. I got to work in earnest.

An Idea Gets Sidetracked

A few months later, however, real-life drama derailed me from my pursuit of invented drama. On a routine trip to America, my sweetheart, Felipe, was detained by a border agent and denied entry to the United States. He had done nothing wrong, but the Department of Homeland Security put him in jail anyway, and then threw him out of the country. We were informed that Felipe could never again come to America—unless we got married. Moreover, if I wanted to be with my love during this stressful and indefinite period of exile, I would have to pack up my entire life immediately and go join him overseas. This I promptly did, and I stayed abroad with him for almost a year as we dealt with our drama and our immigration paperwork.

Such upheaval does not make for the ideal environment in which to devote oneself to writing a sprawling and heavily researched novel about the Brazilian Amazon in the 1960s. Therefore, I put Evelyn away, with sincere promises that I would return to her later, as soon as stability was restored to my life. I put all my existing notes for that novel into storage, along with the rest of my belongings, and then I flew halfway across the planet to be with Felipe and to work on solving our mess. And because I must always be writing about something or else I will go mad, I decided to write about *that*—that is, to chronicle what was going on in my real life, as a way of sorting through its complications and revelations. (As Joan Didion said, "I don't know what I think until I write about it.")

Over time, this experience grew into my memoir *Committed.*

I want to make clear that I do not regret having written *Committed.* I'm forever grateful to that book, as the process of writing it helped me to sort out my extreme anxiety about my impending marriage. But that book commanded my attention for quite a long while, and by the time it was done, more than two years had passed. More than two years that I had not spent working on *Evelyn of the Amazon.*

That's a long time to leave an idea unattended.

I was eager to get back to it. So once Felipe and I were safely married and settled back home in the US, and once *Committed* was finished, I retrieved all my notes out of storage and sat down at my new desk in my new house, ready to recommence crafting my novel about the Amazon jungle.

Right away, however, I made a most distressing discovery.

My novel was gone.

An Idea Goes Away

Allow me to explain.

I do not mean to say that somebody had stolen my notes, or that a crucial computer file had gone missing. What I mean is that the living heart of my novel was gone. The sentient force that inhabits all vibrant creative endeavors had vanished—swallowed like bulldozers in the jungle, you could say. Sure, all the research and writing I'd completed two years earlier was still there, but I knew at once that I was looking at nothing but the empty husk of what had once been a warm and pulsating entity.

I'm pretty stubborn about sticking with projects, so I prodded at the thing for several months, trying to make it work again, hoping to bring it back to life. But it was useless. Nothing was there. It was like poking a stick at a cast-off snakeskin: The more I messed with it, the faster it fell apart and turned to dust.

I believed I knew what had happened, because I'd seen this sort of thing before: The idea had grown tired of waiting, and it had left me. I could scarcely blame it. I had, after all, broken our contract. I'd promised to dedicate myself completely to *Evelyn of the Amazon*, and then I'd reneged on that promise. I hadn't given the book a moment's attention for more than two years. What was the idea supposed to do, sit around indefinitely while I ignored it? Maybe. Sometimes they do wait. Some exceedingly patient ideas might wait years, or even decades, for your attention. But others won't, because each idea has a different nature. Would you sit around in a box for two years while your collaborator blew you off? Probably not.

Thus, the neglected idea did what many self-respecting living entities would do in the same circumstance: It hit the road.

Fair enough, right?

Because this is the other side of the contract with creativity: If inspiration is allowed to unexpectedly enter you, it is also allowed to unexpectedly exit you.

If I'd been younger, the loss of *Evelyn of the Amazon* might have knocked me off my feet, but by this point in my life I'd been in the game of imagination long enough to let it go without excessive struggle. I could have wept over the loss, but I didn't, because I understood the terms of the deal, and I accepted those terms. I understood that the best you can hope for in such a situation is to let your old idea go and catch the *next* idea that comes around. And the best way for that to happen is to move on swiftly, with humility and grace. Don't fall into a funk about the one that got away. Don't beat yourself up. Don't rage at the gods above. All that is nothing but distraction, and the last thing you need is further distraction. Grieve if you must, but grieve efficiently. Better to just say good-bye to the lost idea with dignity and continue onward. Find something else to work on—anything, immediately—and get at it. Keep busy.

Most of all, be ready. Keep your eyes open. Listen. Follow your curiosity. Ask questions. Sniff around. Remain open. Trust in the miraculous truth that new and marvelous ideas are looking for human collaborators every single day. Ideas of every kind are constantly galloping toward us, constantly passing through us, constantly trying to get our attention.

Let them know you're available.

And for heaven's sake, try not to miss the next one.

Wizardry

This should be the end of my Amazon jungle story. But it isn't.

Just around the same time that the idea for my novel ran away—it was now 2008—I made a new friend: Ann

Patchett, the celebrated novelist. We met one afternoon in New York City, on a panel discussion about libraries.

Yes, that's right: a panel discussion about libraries.

The life of a writer is endlessly glamorous.

I was instantly intrigued by Ann, not only because I'd always admired her work, but because she is a rather remarkable presence in person. Ann has a preternatural ability to render herself very small—nearly invisible—in order to better observe the world around her in safe anonymity, so that she can write about it, unnoticed. In other words, her superpower is to conceal her superpowers.

When I first met Ann, then, it is probably not surprising that I didn't immediately recognize her as the famous author. She looked so unassuming and tiny and young that I thought she was somebody's assistant—perhaps even somebody's assistant's assistant. Then I put it together, who she was. I thought, *My goodness! She's so meek!*

But I'd been fooled.

An hour later, Ms. Patchett stood up at the lectern and gave one of the most robust and dazzling speeches I've ever heard. She rocked that room and she rocked me. That's when I realized that this woman was in fact quite tall. And strong. And gorgeous. And passionate. And brilliant. It was as if she'd thrown off her invisibility cloak and a full-on goddess stepped forth.

I was transfixed. I'd never seen anything quite like this complete transformation of presence, from one moment to the next. And because I have no boundaries, I ran up to her after the event and clutched her by the arm, eager to catch this amazing creature before she dematerialized into invisibility again.

I said, "Ann, I realize we've only just met, but I have to tell you—you're extraordinary and I love you!"

Now, Ann Patchett is a woman who actually *does* have boundaries. She looked at me a bit askance, unsurprisingly. She seemed to be deciding something about me. For a moment, I wasn't sure where I stood. But what she did next was wonderful. She cupped my face in her hands and *kissed* me. Then she pronounced, "And I love you, Liz Gilbert."

In that instant, a friendship was ignited.

The terms of our friendship were to be somewhat unusual, though. Ann and I don't live in the same area (I'm in New Jersey; she's in Tennessee), so it wasn't as if we would be able to meet once a week for lunch. Neither of us is a big fan of talking on the phone, either. Nor was social media the place for this relationship to grow. Instead, we decided to get to know each other through the all but lost art of letter-writing.

In a tradition that continues to this day, Ann and I began writing each other long, thoughtful letters every month. Real letters, on real paper, with envelopes and postage and everything. It is a rather antiquated way to be friends with someone, but we are both rather antiquated people. We write about our marriages, our families, our friendships, our frustrations. But mostly we write about *writing*.

Which is how it came to pass that—in the autumn of 2008—Ann casually mentioned in a letter that she had recently begun working on a new novel, and that it was about the Amazon jungle.

For obvious reasons, that caught my attention.

I wrote back and asked Ann what her novel was about, more specifically. I explained that I, too, had been working on an Amazon jungle novel, but that mine had gotten away from me because I'd neglected it (a state of affairs that I knew she would understand). In her next letter, Ann replied that it was too soon yet to know precisely what her jungle novel was about. Early days, still. The story was just taking shape. She would keep me informed as it all evolved.

The following February, Ann and I met in person for only the second time in our lives. We were to appear together onstage at an event in Portland, Oregon. The morning of our appearance, we shared breakfast in the hotel's café. Ann told me that she was now deep into the writing of her new book—more than a hundred pages in.

I said, "Okay, now you really do have to tell me what your Amazon novel is about. I've been dying to know."

"You go first," she said, "since your book was first. You tell me what *your* Amazon jungle novel was about—the one that got away."

I tried to summarize my ex-novel as concisely as possible. I said, "It was about this middle-aged spinster from Minnesota who's been quietly in love with her married boss for many years. He gets involved in a harebrained business scheme down in the Amazon jungle. A bunch of money and a person go missing, and my character gets sent down there to solve things, at which point her quiet life is completely turned into chaos. Also, it's a love story."

Ann stared at me from across the table for a long minute.

Before I continue, I must give you to understand that—decidedly unlike myself—Ann Patchett is a true lady. She has exquisite manners. There is nothing vulgar or coarse about her, which made it even more shocking when she finally spoke:

"You have got to be *fucking* kidding me."

"Why?" I asked. "What's your novel about?"

She replied, "It's about a spinster from Minnesota who's

been quietly in love with her married boss for many years. He gets involved in a harebrained business scheme down in the Amazon jungle. A bunch of money and a person go missing, and my character is sent down there to solve things. At which point her quiet life is completely turned into chaos. Also, it's a love story."

WTF?

That is not a *genre*, people!

That story line is not a Scandinavian murder mystery, or a vampire romance. That is an extremely specific story line. You cannot just go to the bookstore and ask the salesclerk to direct you to the section devoted to books about middle-aged Minnesota spinsters in love with their married bosses who get sent down to the Amazon jungle to find missing people and save doomed projects.

That is not a *thing*!

Admittedly, when we broke it all down to finer details, there were some differences. My novel took place in the 1960s, while Ann's was contemporary. My book had been about the highway construction business, while hers was about the pharmaceutical industry. But other than that? They were the same book.

As you might imagine, it took Ann and me a while to recover our composure after this revelation. Then—like pregnant women eager to recall the exact moment of conception—we each counted backward on our fingers, trying to determine when I had lost the idea and when she had found it.

Turns out, those events had occurred around the same time.

In fact, we think the idea might have been officially transmitted on the day we met.

In fact, we think it was exchanged in the kiss.

And *that*, my friends, is Big Magic.

A Little Perspective

Now, before we get too excited, I want to pause for a moment and ask you to consider all the negative conclusions that I could have drawn about this incident, had I been in the mood to ruin my life.

The worst and most destructive conclusion I could've

drawn was that Ann Patchett had stolen my idea. That would have been absurd, of course, because Ann had never even heard of my idea, and besides, she's the single most ethical human being I've ever met close-up. But people do draw hateful conclusions like this all the time. People convince themselves that they have been robbed when they have not, in fact, been robbed. Such thinking comes from a wretched allegiance to the notion of scarcity—from the belief that the world is a place of dearth, and that there will never be enough of anything to go around. The motto of this mentality is: *Somebody else got mine.* Had I decided to take that attitude, I would surely have lost my dear new friend. I also would have collapsed into a state of resentment, jealousy, and blame.

Alternatively, I could have turned the anger upon myself. I could have said to myself, *See, here's the ultimate proof that you're a loser, Liz, because you never deliver on anything! This novel wanted to be yours, but you blew it, because you suck and you're lazy and you're stupid, and because you always put your attention in the wrong place, and that's why you'll never be great.*

Lastly, I could have put the hate on destiny. I could have said, *Herein lies the evidence that God loves Ann Patchett more than he loves me. For Ann is the chosen novelist and I—as I have always suspected in my darkest moments—am merely a fraud. I am being mocked by fate, while her cup runneth over. I am fortune's fool and she is fortune's darling, and such is the eternal injustice and tragedy of my cursed existence.*

But I didn't do any of that garbage.

Instead, I chose to regard this event as having been a terrific little miracle. I allowed myself to feel grateful and astonished to have played any part whatsoever in its strange unfolding. This was the closest I'd ever felt to sorcery, and I wasn't about to waste that amazing experience by playing small. I saw this incident as a rare and glittering piece of evidence that all my most outlandish beliefs about creativity might actually be true—that ideas *are* alive, that ideas *do* seek the most available human collaborator, that ideas *do* have a conscious will, that ideas *do* move from soul to soul, that ideas *will* always try to seek the swiftest and most efficient conduit to the earth (just as lightning does).

Furthermore, I was now inclined to believe that ideas also have wit, because what had transpired between Ann and me was not only phenomenal, but also curiously and charmingly funny.

Ownership

I believe that inspiration will always try its best to work with you—but if you are not ready or available, it may indeed choose to leave you and to search for a different human collaborator.

This happens to people a lot, actually.

This is how it comes to pass that one morning you open up the newspaper and discover that somebody else has written your book, or directed your play, or released your record, or produced your movie, or founded your business, or launched your restaurant, or patented your invention—or in any way whatsoever manifested some spark of inspiration that you'd had years ago, but had never entirely cultivated, or had never gotten around to finishing. This may vex you, but it really shouldn't, because you didn't deliver! You didn't show up ready enough, or fast enough, or openly enough for the idea to take hold within you and complete itself. Therefore, the idea went hunting for a new partner, and somebody else got to make the thing.

In the years since I published *Eat Pray Love*, I cannot tell you (it is literally beyond my ability to count) how many people have accused me in anger of having written *their* book.

"That book was supposed to be *mine*," they growl, glaring down at me in the signing line at some book event in Houston, or Toronto, or Dublin, or Melbourne. "I was definitely planning to write that book someday. You wrote my life."

But what can I say? What do I know about that stranger's life? From my perspective, I found an unattended idea lying around, and I ran away with it. While it is true that I got lucky with *Eat Pray Love* (without a doubt, I got exceedingly lucky), it is also true that I worked on that book like a maniac. I spun myself like a dervish around that idea. Once it entered my consciousness, I didn't let it out of my sight for a moment—not until the book was good and finished.

So I got to keep that one.

But I've lost a good number of ideas over the years, too—or, rather, I've lost ideas that I mistakenly thought were meant to be mine. Other people got to write books that I dearly longed to write. Other people made projects that might have been mine.

Here's one: In 2006, I toyed for a while with the idea of writing a sprawling nonfiction history of Newark, New

Jersey, and to call it *Brick City*. My notional plan was to follow around Newark's charismatic new mayor, Cory Booker, and to write about his efforts to transform this fascinating but troubled town. A cool idea, but I didn't get around to it. (To be honest, it seemed like a lot of work, and I had another book already brewing, so I never quite revved up enough juice to take it on.) Then, in 2009, the Sundance Channel produced and aired a sprawling documentary about the troubled history of Newark, New Jersey, and about Cory Booker's efforts to turn the town around. The show was called *Brick City*. My reaction upon hearing this was one of sheer relief: *Hooray! I don't have to tackle Newark! Someone else took on the assignment!*

Here's another one: In 1996, I met a guy who was a good friend of Ozzy Osbourne's. He told me that the Osbourne family were the strangest, funniest, wildest, and most oddly loving people he had ever met. He said, "You've gotta write something about them! You should just hang out with them and watch the way they interact. I don't know exactly what you should do about them, but *somebody* has to do a project around the Osbournes, because they're too fantastic to believe."

I was intrigued. But, again, I never got around to it, and somebody else ended up taking on the Osbournes—to noteworthy effect.

There are so many ideas that I never got around to, and often they became someone else's projects. Other people told stories that were intimately familiar to me—stories that had once been called to my attention, or seemed to come from my own life, or could have been generated by my imagination. Sometimes I haven't been so nonchalant about losing those ideas to other creators. Sometimes it's been painful. Sometimes I've had to watch as other people enjoyed successes and victories that I once desired for myself.

Them's the breaks, though.

But them's also the beautiful mysteries.

Multiple Discovery

When I contemplated things even further, I realized that what had transpired between me and Ann Patchett could have been the artistic version of multiple discovery—a term used in the scientific community whenever two or more scientists in different parts of the world come up with the same idea at the same time. (Calculus, oxygen, black holes, the Möbius strip, the existence of the stratosphere, and the theory of evolution—to name just a few—all had multiple discoverers.)

There's no logical explanation for why this occurs. How can two people who have never heard of each other's work both arrive at the same scientific conclusions at the same historical moment? Yet it happens more often than you might imagine. When the nineteenth-century Hungarian mathematician János Bolyai invented non-Euclidean geometry, his father urged him to publish his findings immediately, before someone else landed on the same idea, saying, "When the time is ripe for certain things, they appear at different places, in the manner of violets coming to light in early spring."

Multiple discovery happens outside the scientific sphere, too. In the business world, for instance, there's a general understanding that a big new idea is "out there," floating around in the atmosphere, and that the first person or company to grab hold of it will likewise seize the competitive advantage. Sometimes everyone's grabbing at once, in a mad scramble to be first. (See: the rise of personal computers in the 1990s.)

Multiple discovery even happens in romantic relationships. Nobody's been interested in you for years and years, and suddenly you have two suitors at the same time? That's multiple discovery, indeed!

To me, multiple discovery just looks like inspiration

hedging its bets, fiddling with the dials, working two channels at the same time. Inspiration is allowed to do that, if it wants to. Inspiration is allowed to do whatever it wants to, in fact, and it is never obliged to justify its motives to any of us. (As far as I'm concerned, we're lucky that inspiration talks to us at all; it's too much to ask that it also explain itself.)

In the end, it's all just violets trying to come to light.

Don't fret about the irrationality and unpredictability of all this strangeness. Give in to it. Such is the bizarre, unearthly contract of creative living. There is no theft; there is no ownership; there is no tragedy; there is no problem. There is no time or space where inspiration comes from—and also no competition, no ego, no limitations. There is only the stubbornness of the idea itself, refusing to stop searching until it has found an equally stubborn collaborator. (Or multiple collaborators, as the case may be.)

Work with that stubbornness.

Work with it as openly and trustingly and diligently as you can.

Work with all your heart, because—I promise—if you show up for your work day after day after day after day, you just might get lucky enough some random morning to burst right into bloom.

The Tiger's Tail

One of the best descriptions I've ever heard of this phenomenon—that is, of ideas entering and exiting the human consciousness at whim—came from the wonderful American poet Ruth Stone.

I met Stone when she was nearly ninety years old, and she regaled me with stories about her extraordinary creative process. She told me that when she was a child growing up on a farm in rural Virginia, she would be out working in the fields when she would sometimes *hear* a poem coming toward her—hear it rushing across the landscape at her, like a galloping horse. Whenever this happened, she knew exactly what she had to do next: She would "run like hell" toward the house, trying to stay ahead of the poem, hoping to get to a piece of paper and a pencil fast enough to catch it. That way, when the poem reached her and passed through her, she would be able to grab it and take dictation, letting the words pour forth onto the page. Sometimes, however, she was too slow, and she couldn't get to the paper and pencil in time. At those instances, she could feel the poem rushing right through her body and out the other side. It would be in her for a moment, seeking a response, and then it would be gone before she could grasp it—galloping away across the earth, as she said, "searching for another poet."

But sometimes (and this is the wildest part) she would *nearly* miss the poem, but not quite. She would just barely catch it, she explained, "by the tail." Like grabbing a tiger. Then she would almost physically *pull* the poem back into her with one hand, even as she was taking dictation with the other. In these instances, the poem would appear on the page from the last word to the first—backward, but otherwise intact.

That, my friends, is some freaky, old-timey, voodoo-style Big Magic, right there.

I believe in it, though.

•

Hard Labor vs. Fairy Dust

I believe in it, because I believe we are all capable at times of brushing up against a sense of mystery and inspiration in our lives. Maybe we can't all be pure divine channels like Ruth Stone, pouring forth unadulterated creation every single day without obstacle or doubt . . . but we may be able to draw nearer to that source than we think.

Most of my writing life, to be perfectly honest, is not freaky, old-timey, voodoo-style Big Magic. Most of my writing life consists of nothing more than unglamorous, disciplined labor. I sit at my desk and I work like a farmer, and that's how it gets done. Most of it is not fairy dust in the least.

But sometimes it *is* fairy dust. Sometimes, when I'm in the midst of writing, I feel like I am suddenly walking on one of those moving sidewalks that you find in a big airport terminal; I still have a long slog to my gate, and my baggage is still heavy, but I can feel myself being gently propelled by some exterior force. Something is carrying me along—something powerful and generous—and that something is decidedly not *me*.

You may know this feeling. It's the feeling you get when you've made something wonderful, or done something wonderful, and when you look back at it later, all you can say is: "I don't even know where that came from."

You can't repeat it. You can't explain it. But it felt as if you were being guided.

I only rarely experience this feeling, but it's the most magnificent sensation imaginable when it arrives. I don't think there is a more perfect happiness to be found in life than this state, except perhaps falling in love. In ancient Greek, the word for the highest degree of human happiness is *eudaimonia*, which basically means "well-daemoned"—that is, nicely taken care of by some external divine creative spirit guide. (Modern commentators, perhaps uncomfortable with this sense of divine mystery, simply call it "flow" or "being in the zone.")

But the Greeks and the Romans both believed in the idea of an external daemon of creativity—a sort of house elf, if you will, who lived within the walls of your home and who sometimes aided you in your labors. The Romans had a specific term for that helpful house elf. They called it your genius—your guardian deity, the conduit of your inspiration. Which is to say, the Romans didn't believe that an exceptionally gifted person *was* a genius; they believed that an exceptionally gifted person *had* a genius.

It's a subtle but important distinction (being vs. having) and, I think, it's a wise psychological construct. The idea of an external genius helps to keep the artist's ego in check, distancing him somewhat from the burden of taking either full credit or full blame for the outcome of his work. If your work is successful, in other words, you are obliged to thank your external genius for the help, thus holding you back from total narcissism. And if your work fails, it's not entirely your fault. You can say, "Hey, don't look at me—my genius didn't show up today!"

Either way, the vulnerable human ego is protected.

Protected from the corrupting influence of praise.

Protected from the corrosive effects of shame.

Pinned Beneath the Boulder

I think society did a great disservice to artists when we started saying that certain people *were* geniuses, instead of saying they *had* geniuses. That happened around the Renaissance, with the rise of a more rational and human-centered view of life. The gods and the mysteries fell away, and suddenly we put all the credit and blame for creativity on the artists themselves—making the all-too-fragile humans completely responsible for the vagaries of inspiration.

In the process, we also venerated art and artists beyond their appropriate stations. The distinction of "being a genius" (and the rewards and status often associated with it) elevated creators into something like a priestly caste—perhaps even into minor deities—which I think is a bit too much pressure for mere mortals, no matter how talented. That's when artists start to really crack, driven mad and broken in half by the weight and weirdness of their gifts.

When artists are burdened with the label of "genius," I think they lose the ability to take themselves lightly, or to create freely. Consider Harper Lee, for instance, who wrote nothing for decades after the phenomenonal success of *To Kill a Mockingbird.* In 1962, when Lee was asked how she felt about the possibility of ever writing another book, she replied, "I'm scared." She also said, "When you're at the top, there's only one way to go."

Because Lee never elaborated more definitively on her situation, we will never know why this wildly successful author didn't go on to write dozens more books in her lifetime. But I wonder if perhaps she had become pinned beneath the boulder of her own reputation. Maybe it all got too heavy, too freighted with responsibility, and her artistry died of fear—or worse, self-competition. (What was there for Harper Lee to be afraid of, after all? Possibly just this: That she could not outdo Harper Lee.)

As for having reached the top, with only one way to go from there, Lee had a point, no? I mean, if you cannot repeat a once-in-a-lifetime miracle—if you can never again reach the top—then why bother creating at all? Well, I can actually speak about this predicament from personal experience, because I myself was once "at the top"—with a book that sat on the bestseller list for more than three years. I can't tell you how many people said to me during those years, "How are you ever going to top that?" They'd speak of my great good fortune as though it were a curse, not a blessing, and would speculate about how terrified I must feel at the prospect of not being able to reach such phenomenal heights again.

But such thinking assumes there is a "top"—and that reaching that top (and staying there) is the only motive one has to create. Such thinking assumes that the mysteries of inspiration operate on the same scale that we do—on a limited human scale of success and failure, of winning and losing, of comparison and competition, of commerce and reputation, of units sold and influence wielded. Such thinking assumes that you must be constantly victorious—not only against your peers, but also against an earlier version of your own poor self. Most dangerously of all, such thinking assumes that if you cannot win, then you must not continue to play.

But what does any of that have to do with vocation? What does any of that have to do with the pursuit of love? What does any of that have to do with the strange communion between the human and the magical? What does any of that have to do with faith? What does any of that have to do with the quiet glory of merely *making things*, and then sharing those things with an open heart and no expectations?

I wish that Harper Lee had kept writing. I wish that, right after *Mockingbird* and her Pulitzer Prize, she had churned out five cheap and easy books in a row—a light romance, a police procedural, a children's story, a cookbook, some kind of pulpy action-adventure story, *anything*. You might think I'm kidding, but I'm not. Imagine what she might have created, even accidentally, with such an approach. At the very least, she could have tricked everyone into forgetting that she'd once been Harper Lee. She could have tricked *herself* into forgetting that she'd once been Harper Lee, which might have been artistically liberating.

Fortunately, after so many decades of silence, we do get to hear more of Lee's voice. Recently, a lost early manuscript of hers was discovered—a novel that she wrote before *To Kill a Mockingbird* (in other words: a book that she wrote before the entire world was watching and waiting for what she would do next, hovering with expectation). But I wish someone had been able to convince Lee to keep writing for the entirety of her life, and to keep publishing all along. It would have been a gift to the world. And it would have been a gift to her, as well—to have been able to remain a writer, and to have enjoyed the pleasures and satisfactions of that work for herself (because in the end, creativity is a gift to the creator, not just a gift to the audience).

I wish somebody had given Ralph Ellison the same sort of advice. Just write anything and put it out there with reckless abandon. And F. Scott Fitzgerald, too. And any other creator, famous or obscure, who ever vanished beneath the shadow of their own real or imagined reputation. I wish somebody had told them all to go fill up a bunch of pages with *blah-blah-blah* and just publish it, for heaven's sake, and ignore the outcome.

Does it seem sacrilegious even to suggest this?

Good.

Just because creativity is mystical doesn't mean it shouldn't also be demystified—especially if it means liberating artists from the confines of their own grandiosity, panic, and ego.

Let It Come and Go

The most important thing to understand about *eudaimonia*, though—about that exhilarating encounter between a human being and divine creative inspiration—is that you cannot expect it to be there for you all the time.

It will come and go, and you must let it come and go.

I know this personally, because my genius—wherever it comes from—does not keep regular hours. My genius, for what he is worth, does not work on human time and he certainly doesn't arrange his schedule around my convenience. Sometimes I suspect that my genius might be moonlighting on the side as somebody else's genius—maybe even working for a bunch of different artists, like some kind of freelance creative contractor. Sometimes I grope around in the dark, desperately looking for magical creative stimulus, and all I come up with is something that feels like a damp washcloth.

And then suddenly—*whoosh!*—inspiration arrives, out of the clear blue sky.

And then—*whoosh!*—it is gone again.

I once took a nap on a commuter train, and while I was asleep, I dreamed an entire short story, absolutely intact. I awoke from my dream, grabbed a pen, and wrote down that story in one fevered burst of inspiration. This was the closest I've ever come to having a pure Ruth Stone moment. Some channel opened wide within me, and the words poured forth for page after page without any effort whatsoever.

When I finished writing that short story, I barely had to revise a word of it. It felt right just the way it was. It felt right, and it felt *strange*; it wasn't even the kind of thing I would normally write about. Several reviewers later took note of how different that story was from the others in my collection. (One critic, tellingly, described it as "Yankee Magic Realism.") It was a tale of enchantment, written under enchantment, and even a stranger could feel the fairy dust in it. I've never written anything like it before or since. I still think of that short story as the most superbly formed hidden jewel I've ever unburied in myself.

That was Big Magic at play, unmistakably.

But that was also twenty-two years ago, and it has never happened again. (And believe me, I've taken a lot of naps on a lot of trains in the meantime.) I've had moments of wondrous creative communion since then, but nothing so pure and exhilarating as that one wild encounter.

It came, and then it went.

What I'm saying is this: If my plan is to sit around waiting for another such unadulterated and impassioned creative visitation, I may be waiting for a very long time. So I don't sit around waiting to write until my genius decides to pay me a visit. If anything, I have come to believe that my genius spends a lot of time waiting around for *me*—waiting to see if I'm truly serious about this line of work. I feel sometimes like my genius sits in the corner and watches me at my desk, day after day, week after week, month after month, just to be sure I really mean it, just to be sure I'm really giving this creative endeavor my whole-hearted effort. When my genius is convinced that I'm not just messing around here, he may show up and offer assistance. Sometimes that assistance will not arrive until two years into a project. Sometimes that assistance will not last for more than ten minutes.

When that assistance does arrive—that sense of the moving sidewalk beneath my feet, the moving sidewalk beneath my *words*—I am delighted, and I go along for the ride. In such instances, I write like I am not quite myself. I lose track of time and space and self. While it's happening, I thank the mystery for its help. And when it departs, I let the mystery go, and I keep on working diligently anyhow, hoping that someday my genius will reappear.

I work either way, you see—assisted or unassisted—because that is what you must do in order to live a fully creative life. I work steadily, and I always thank the process. Whether I am touched by grace or not, I thank creativity for allowing me to engage with it at all.

Because either way, it's all kind of amazing—what we get to do, what we get to attempt, what we *sometimes* get to commune with.

Gratitude, always.

Always, gratitude.

A Dazzled Heart

And as for how Ann Patchett saw what had happened between us?

As for how she regarded our curious miracle, about the Amazon jungle novel that had bounced out of my head and landed in hers?

Well, Ann is a far more rational soul than I am, but even she felt that something rather supernatural had occurred. Even she felt that inspiration had slipped away from me and landed—with a kiss—upon her. In her subsequent letters to me, she was generous enough to always refer to her Amazon jungle novel as "our Amazon jungle novel," as though she were the surrogate mother to an idea that I had conceived.

That was gracious of her, but not at all true. As anyone who has ever read *State of Wonder* knows full well, that magnificent story is entirely Ann Patchett's. Nobody else could have written that novel as she wrote it. If anything, *I* had been the foster mother who'd kept the idea warm for a couple of years while it searched for its true and rightful collaborator. Who knows how many other writers that idea had visited over the years before it came into my care for a while, and then finally shifted over to Ann? (Boris Pasternak described this phenomenon beautifully, when he wrote, "No genuine book has a first page. Like the rustling of the forest, it is begotten God knows where, and it grows and it rolls, arousing the dense wilds of the forest until suddenly . . . it begins to speak with all the treetops at once.")

All I know for certain is that this novel really wanted to be written, and it didn't stop its rolling search until it finally found the author who was ready and willing to take it on—not later, not someday, not in a few years, not when times get better, not when life becomes easier, but *right now.*

So that became Ann's story.

Which left me with nothing but a dazzled heart and the sense that I live in a most remarkable world, thick with mysteries. It all called to mind the British physicist Sir Arthur Eddington's memorable explanation of how the universe works: "Something unknown is doing we don't know what."

But the best part is: *I don't need to know what.*

I don't demand a translation of the unknown. I don't need to understand what it all means, or where ideas are originally conceived, or why creativity plays out as unpredictably as it does. I don't need to know why we are sometimes able to converse freely with inspiration, when at other times we labor hard in solitude and come up with nothing. I don't need to know why an idea visited you today and not me. Or why it visited us both. Or why it abandoned us both.

None of us can know such things, for these are among the great enigmas.

All I know for certain is that *this is how I want to spend my life*—collaborating to the best of my ability with forces of inspiration that I can neither see, nor prove, nor command, nor understand.

It's a strange line of work, admittedly.

I cannot think of a better way to pass my days.

Permission

Remove the Suggestion Box

I didn't grow up in a family of artists.

I come from people who worked more regularly at life, you might say.

My maternal grandfather was a dairy farmer; my paternal grandfather was a furnace salesman. Both my grandmothers were housewives, and so were their mothers, their sisters, their aunts.

As for my parents, my father is an engineer and my mother is a nurse. And although they were the right age for it, my parents were never hippies—not in the least. They were far too conservative for such things. My dad spent the 1960s in college and the Navy; my mom spent those same years in nursing school, working night shifts at the hospital, and responsibly saving her money. After they were married, my dad got a job at a chemical company, and he worked there for thirty years. Mom worked part-time, became an active member of our local church, served on the school board, volunteered at the library, and visited the elderly and the housebound.

They were responsible people. Taxpayers. Solid. Voted for Reagan. (Twice!)

I learned how to be a rebel from them.

Because—just beyond the reach of their basic good citizenship—my parents did whatever the hell they wanted to do with their lives, and they did it with a rather fabulous sense of insouciance. My father decided that he didn't merely want to be a chemical engineer; he also wanted to be a Christmas-tree farmer, and so in 1973 he went and did that. He moved us out to a farm, cleared some land, planted some seedlings, and commenced with his project. He didn't quit his day job to follow his dream; he just folded his dream into his everyday life. He wanted to raise goats, too, so he acquired some goats. Brought them home in the backseat of our Ford Pinto. Had he ever raised goats? No, but he thought he could figure it out. It was the same thing when he became interested in beekeeping: He just got himself some bees and began. Thirty-five years later, he still has those hives.

When my father grew curious about things, he pursued them. He had solid faith in his own capabilities. And when my father needed something (which was rare, because he basically has the material needs of a hobo), he made it himself, or fixed it himself, or somehow cobbled it together himself—usually without referring to the instructions, and generally without asking the advice of an expert. My dad doesn't hold much respect for instructions or for experts. He is no more impressed by people's degrees than he is by other civilized niceties such as building permits and NO TRESPASSING signs. (For better or for worse, my dad taught me that the best place to pitch a tent will always be the spot marked NO CAMPING.)

My father *really* doesn't like being told what to do. His sense of individualistic defiance is so strong, it's often comical. Back in the Navy, he was once commanded by his captain to make a suggestion box to put in the canteen. Dad dutifully built the box, nailed it to the wall, then wrote the first suggestion and dropped it through the slot. His note read: *I suggest that you remove the suggestion box.*

In many ways he's a weird egg, my dad, and his hyperantiauthoritarian instincts can border at times on the pathological . . . but I always suspected that he was kind of cool, anyway, even back when I was an easily embarrassed child being driven around town in a Ford Pinto filled with goats. I knew that he was doing his own thing and following his own path, and I intuitively sensed that this made him, by definition, an interesting person. I didn't have a term for it back then, but I can see now that he was practicing something called creative living.

I liked it.

I also took note of it for when it came time to imagine my own life. It's not that I wanted to make any of the same choices my father had made (I am neither a farmer nor a Republican), but his example empowered me to forge my own way through the world however I liked. Also, just like my dad, I don't like people telling me what to do. While I am not at all confrontational, I am deeply stubborn. This stubbornness helps when it comes to the business of creative living.

As for my mother, she's a slightly more civilized version of my dad. Her hair is always neat, and her kitchen is tidy, and her friendly good Midwestern manners are impeccable, but don't underestimate her, because her will is made of titanium and her talents are vast. She's a woman who always believed that she could build, sew, grow, knit, mend, patch, paint, or decoupage anything her family ever needed. She cut our hair. She baked our bread. She grew, harvested, and preserved our vegetables. She made our clothes. She birthed our baby goats. She slaughtered the chickens, then served them up for dinner. She wallpapered our living room herself, and she refinished our piano (which she had bought for fifty bucks from a local church). She saved us trips to the doctor by patching us up on her own. She smiled sweetly at everyone and always acted like a total cooperator—but then she shaped her own world exactly to her liking while nobody was looking.

I think it was my parents' example of quietly impudent self-assertion that gave me the idea that I could be a writer, or at least that I could go out there and *try*. I never recall my parents expressing any worry whatsoever at my dream of becoming a writer. If they did worry, they kept quiet about it—but honestly, I don't think they were concerned. I think they had faith that I would always be able to take care of myself, because they had taught me to. (Anyhow, the golden rule in my family is this: If you're supporting yourself financially and you're not bothering anyone else, then you're free to do whatever you want with your life.)

Maybe because they didn't worry too much about me, I didn't worry too much about me, either.

It also never occurred to me to go ask an authority figure for permission to become a writer. I'd never seen anybody in my family ask anyone for permission to do *anything*.

They just made stuff.

So that's what I decided to do: I decided to just go make stuff.

Your Permission Slip

Here's what I'm getting at, dear ones:

You do not need anybody's permission to live a creative life.

Maybe you didn't receive this kind of message when you were growing up. Maybe your parents were terrified of risk in any form. Maybe your parents were obsessive-compulsive rule-followers, or maybe they were too busy being melancholic depressives, or addicts, or abusers to ever use their imaginations toward creativity. Maybe they were afraid of what the neighbors would say. Maybe your parents weren't makers in the least. Maybe they were pure consumers. Maybe you grew up in an environment where people just sat around watching TV and waiting for stuff to happen to them.

Forget about it. It doesn't matter.

Look a little further back in your family's history. Look at your grandparents: Odds are pretty good *they* were makers. No? Not yet? Keep looking back, then. Go back further still. Look at your great-grandparents. Look at your ancestors. Look at the ones who were immigrants, or slaves, or soldiers, or farmers, or sailors, or the original people who watched the ships arrive with the strangers onboard. Go back far enough and you will find people who were not consumers, people who were not sitting around passively waiting for stuff to happen to them. You will find people who spent their lives making things.

This is where you come from.

This is where we all come from.

Human beings have been creative beings for a really long time—long enough and consistently enough that it appears to be a totally natural impulse. To put the story in perspective, consider this fact: The earliest evidence of recognizable human art is forty thousand years old. The earliest evidence of human agriculture, by contrast, is only ten thousand years old. Which means that somewhere in our collective evolutionary story, we decided it was way more important to make attractive, superfluous items than it was to learn how to regularly feed ourselves.

The diversity in our creative expression is fantastic. Some of the most enduring and beloved artwork on earth is unmistakably majestic. Some of it makes you want to drop to your knees and weep. Some of it doesn't, though. Some acts of artistic expression might stir and excite you, but bore me to death. Some of the art that people have created across the centuries is absolutely sublime, and probably did emerge from a grand sense of seriousness and sacredness, but a lot of it didn't. A lot of it is just folks messing around for their own diversion—making their pottery a little prettier, or building a nicer chair, or drawing penises on walls to pass the time. And that's fine, too.

You want to write a book? Make a song? Direct a movie? Decorate pottery? Learn a dance? Explore a new land? You want to draw a penis on your wall? Do it. Who cares? It's your birthright as a human being, so do it with a cheerful heart. (I mean, take it seriously, sure—but don't take it *seriously*.) Let inspiration lead you wherever it wants to lead you. Keep in mind that for most of history people just made things, and they didn't make such a big freaking deal out of it.

We make things because we *like* making things.

We pursue the interesting and the novel because we *like* the interesting and the novel.

And inspiration works with us, it seems, because inspiration *likes* working us—because human beings are possessed of something special, something extra, something unnecessarily rich, something that the novelist Marilynne Robinson calls "an overabundance that is magical."

That magical overabundance?

That's your inherent creativity, humming and stirring quietly in its deep reserve.

Are you considering becoming a creative person? Too late, you already are one. To even call somebody "a creative person" is almost laughably redundant; creativity is the hallmark of our species. We have the senses for it; we have the curiosity for it; we have the opposable thumbs for it; we have the rhythm for it; we have the language and the excitement and the innate connection to divinity for it.

If you're alive, you're a creative person. You and I and everyone you know are descended from tens of thousands of years of makers. Decorators, tinkerers, storytellers, dancers, explorers, fiddlers, drummers, builders, growers, problem-solvers, and embellishers—these are our common ancestors.

The guardians of high culture will try to convince you that the arts belong only to a chosen few, but they are wrong and they are also annoying. We are *all* the chosen few. We are all makers by design. Even if you grew up watching cartoons in a sugar stupor from dawn to dusk, creativity still lurks within you. Your creativity is way older than you are, way older than any of us. Your very body and your very being are perfectly designed to live in collaboration with inspiration, and inspiration is still trying to find you—the same way it hunted down your ancestors.

All of which is to say: *You do not need a permission slip from the principal's office to live a creative life.*

Or if you do worry that you need a permission slip—THERE, I just gave it to you.

I just wrote it on the back of an old shopping list.

Consider yourself fully accredited.

Now go make something.

Decorate Yourself

I have a neighbor who gets tattoos all the time.

Her name is Eileen. She acquires new tattoos the way I might acquire a new pair of cheap earrings—just for the heck of it, just on a whim. She wakes up some mornings in a funk and announces, "I think I'll go get a new tattoo today." If you ask Eileen what kind of tattoo she's planning on getting, she'll say, "Oh, I dunno. I'll figure it out when I get to the tattoo shop. Or I'll just let the artist surprise me."

Now, this woman is not a teenager with impulse-control issues. She's a grown woman, with adult children, who runs a successful business. She's also very cool, uniquely gorgeous, and one of the most free spirits I've ever met. When

I asked her once how she could allow her body to be marked up so casually with permanent ink, she said, "Oh, but you misunderstand! It's not permanent. It's just temporary."

Confused, I asked, "You mean, all your tattoos are temporary?"

She smiled and said, "No, Liz. My tattoos are permanent; it's just my *body* that's temporary. So is yours. We're only here on earth for a short while, so I decided a long time ago that I wanted to decorate myself as playfully as I can, while I still have time."

I love this so much, I can't even tell you.

Because—like Eileen—I also want to live the most vividly decorated temporary life that I can. I don't just mean physically; I mean emotionally, spiritually, intellectually. I don't want to be afraid of bright colors, or new sounds, or big love, or risky decisions, or strange experiences, or weird endeavors, or sudden changes, or even failure.

Mind you, I'm not going to go out and cover myself with tattoos (simply because that doesn't happen to be my jam), but I *am* going to spend as much time as I can creating delightful things out of my existence, because that's what brings me awake and that's what brings me alive.

I do my decorating with printer ink, not with tattoo ink. But my urge to write comes from exactly the same place as

Eileen's urge to turn her skin into a vivid canvas while she's still here.

It comes from a place of *Hey, why not?*

Because it's all just temporary.

Entitlement

But in order to live this way—free to create, free to explore—you must possess a fierce sense of personal entitlement, which I hope you will learn to cultivate.

I recognize that the word *entitlement* has dreadfully negative connotations, but I'd like to appropriate it here and put it to good use, because you will never be able to create anything interesting out of your life if you don't believe that you're entitled to at least try. Creative entitlement doesn't mean behaving like a princess, or acting as though the world owes you anything whatsoever. No, creative entitlement simply means believing that *you are allowed to be here*, and that—merely by being here—you are allowed to have a voice and a vision of your own.

The poet David Whyte calls this sense of creative entitlement "the arrogance of belonging," and claims that it is an absolutely vital privilege to cultivate if you wish to interact more vividly with life. Without this arrogance of belonging, you will never be able to take any creative risks whatsoever. Without it, you will never push yourself out of the suffocating insulation of personal safety and into the frontiers of the beautiful and the unexpected.

The arrogance of belonging is not about egotism or self-absorption. In a strange way, it's the opposite; it is a divine force that will actually *take you out of yourself* and allow you to engage more fully with life. Because often what keeps you from creative living *is* your self-absorption (your self-doubt, your self-disgust, your self-judgment, your crushing sense of self-protection). The arrogance of belonging pulls you out of the darkest depths of self-hatred—not by saying "I am the greatest!" but merely by saying "I am here!"

I believe that this good kind of arrogance—this simple entitlement to exist, and therefore to express yourself—is the only weapon with which to combat the nasty dialogue that may automatically arise within your head whenever you get an artistic impulse. You know the nasty dialogue I mean, right? I'm talking about the nasty dialogue that goes like this: "Who the hell do you think you are, trying to be creative? You suck, you're stupid, you have no talent, and you serve no purpose. Get back in your hole."

To which you may have spent a lifetime obediently

responding, "You're right. I do suck and I am stupid. Thank you. I'll go back in my hole now."

I would like to see you engaged in a more generative and interesting conversation with yourself than that. For heaven's sake, at least defend yourself!

Defending yourself as a creative person begins by defining yourself. It begins when you declare your intent. Stand up tall and say it aloud, whatever it is:

I'm a writer.
I'm a singer.
I'm an actor.
I'm a gardener.
I'm a dancer.
I'm an inventor.
I'm a photographer.
I'm a chef.
I'm a designer.
I am this, and I am that, and I am also this other thing, too!
I don't yet know exactly what I am, but I'm curious enough to go find out!

Speak it. Let it know you're there. Hell, let *you* know you're there—because this statement of intent is just as much an announcement to yourself as it is an announcement to the universe or anybody else. Hearing this announcement, your soul will mobilize accordingly. It will mobilize *ecstatically*, in fact, because this is what your soul was born for. (Trust me, your soul has been waiting for you to wake up to your own existence for years.)

But you must be the one to start that conversation, and then you must feel entitled to stay in that conversation.

This proclamation of intent and entitlement is not something you can do just once and then expect miracles; it's something you must do daily, forever. I've had to keep defining and defending myself as a writer every single day of my adult life—constantly reminding and re-reminding my soul and the cosmos that I'm very serious about the business of creative living, and that I will never stop creating, no matter what the outcome, and no matter how deep my anxieties and insecurities may be.

Over time, I've found the right tone of voice for these assertions, too. It's best to be insistent, but affable. Repeat yourself, but don't get shrill. Speak to your darkest and most negative interior voices the way a hostage negotiator speaks to a violent psychopath: calmly, but firmly. Most of all, never back down. You cannot afford to back down. The life you are negotiating to save, after all, is your own.

"Who the hell do you think you are?" your darkest interior voices will demand.

"It's funny you should ask," you can reply. "I'll tell you who I am: I am a child of God, just like anyone else. I am a constituent of this universe. I have invisible spirit benefactors who believe in me, and who labor alongside me. The fact that I am here at all is evidence that I have the right to be here. I have a right to my own voice and a right to my own vision. I have a right to collaborate with creativity, because I myself am a product and a consequence of Creation. I'm on a mission of artistic liberation, *so let the girl go*."

See?

Now you're the one doing the talking.

Originality vs. Authenticity

Maybe you fear that you are not original enough.

Maybe that's the problem—you're worried that your ideas are commonplace and pedestrian, and therefore unworthy of creation.

Aspiring writers will often tell me, "I have an idea, but I'm afraid it's already been done."

Well, yes, it probably has already been done. Most things have already been done—but they have not yet been done by *you.*

By the time Shakespeare was finished with his run on life, he'd pretty much covered every story line there is, but that hasn't stopped nearly five centuries of writers from exploring the same story lines all over again. (And remember, many of those stories were already clichés long before even Shakespeare got his hands on them.) When Picasso saw the ancient cave paintings at Lascaux, he reportedly said, "We have learned nothing in twelve thousand years"—which is probably true, but so what?

So what if we repeat the same themes? So what if we circle around the same ideas, again and again, generation after generation? So what if every new generation feels the same urges and asks the same questions that humans have been feeling and asking for years? We're all related, after all, so there's going to be some repetition of creative instinct. Everything reminds us of something. But once you put your own expression and passion behind an idea, that idea becomes *yours.*

Anyhow, the older I get, the less impressed I become

with originality. These days, I'm far more moved by authenticity. Attempts at originality can often feel forced and precious, but authenticity has quiet resonance that never fails to stir me.

Just say what you want to say, then, and say it with all your heart.

Share whatever you are driven to share.

If it's authentic enough, believe me—it will *feel* original.

Motives

Oh, and here's another thing: You are not required to save the world with your creativity.

Your art not only doesn't have to be original, in other words; it also doesn't have to be *important.*

For example: Whenever anybody tells me they want to write a book in order to help other people, I always think, *Oh, please don't.*

Please don't try to help me.

I mean, it is very kind of you to want to help people, but please don't make it your sole creative motive, because we will feel the weight of your heavy intention, and it will put a strain upon our souls. (It reminds me of this wonderful adage from the British columnist Katharine Whitehorn: "You can recognize the people who live for others by the haunted look on the faces of the others.") I would so much rather that you wrote a book in order to entertain yourself than to help me. Or if your subject matter is darker and more serious, I would prefer that you made your art in order to save yourself, or to relieve yourself of some great psychic burden, rather than to save or relieve *us.*

I once wrote a book in order to save myself. I wrote a travel memoir in order to make sense of my own journey and my own emotional confusion. All I was trying to do with that book was figure myself out. In the process, though, I wrote a story that apparently helped a lot of other people figure themselves out—but that was never my intention. If I'd sat down to write *Eat Pray Love* with the sole aim of helping others, I would've produced an entirely different book. I might have even produced a book that was insufferably unreadable. (Okay, okay . . . Admittedly a lot of critics found *Eat Pray Love* insufferably unreadable as it was—but that's not my point: My point is that I wrote that book for my own purposes, and maybe that's why it felt genuine, and ultimately even helpful, to many readers.)

Consider this very book, for example, which you are right now holding in your hands. *Big Magic* is obviously a self-help guide, right? But with all due respect and affection,

I did not write this book for you; I wrote it for *me*. I wrote this book for my own pleasure, because I truly enjoy thinking about the subject of creativity. It's enjoyable and useful for me to meditate on this topic. If what I've written here ends up helping you, that's great, and I will be glad. That would be a wonderful side effect. But at the end of the day, I do what I do because I like doing it.

I have a friend who's a nun who has spent her entire life working to help the homeless of Philadelphia. She is something close to a living saint. She is a tireless advocate for the poor and the suffering and the lost and the abandoned. And do you know why her charitable outreach is so effective? *Because she likes doing it.* Because it's enjoyable for her. Otherwise it wouldn't work. Otherwise, it would just be hard duty and grim martyrdom. But Sister Mary Scullion is no martyr. She's a cheerful soul who's having a wonderful time living out the existence that best suits her nature and most brings her to life. It just so happens that she takes care of a lot of other people in the process—but everyone can sense her genuine enjoyment behind the mission, which is ultimately why her presence is so healing.

It's okay if your work is fun for you, is what I'm saying. It's also okay if your work is healing for you, or fascinating for you, or redemptive for you, or if it's maybe just a hobby that keeps you from going crazy. It's even okay if your work is totally frivolous. That's allowed. It's all allowed.

Your own reasons to create are reason enough. Merely by pursuing what you love, you may inadvertently end up helping us plenty. ("There is no love which does not become help," taught the theologian Paul Tillich.) Do whatever brings you to life, then. Follow your own fascinations, obsessions, and compulsions. Trust them. Create whatever causes a revolution in your heart.

The rest of it will take care of itself.

Schooling

I never got an advanced degree in writing. I don't have an advanced degree in anything, actually. I graduated from NYU with a bachelor's degree in political science (because you have to major in *something*) and I still feel lucky to have received what I consider to have been an excellent, old-fashioned, broad-minded liberal arts education.

While I always knew that I wanted to be a writer, and while I took a few writing classes as an undergrad, I chose not to seek out a master's of fine arts in creative writing once I was finished at NYU. I was suspicious of the idea that the best place for me to find my voice would be in a room filled with fifteen other young writers trying to find *their* voices.

Also, I wasn't exactly sure what an advanced degree in creative writing would afford me. Going to an arts school is not like going to dentistry school, for instance, where you can be pretty certain of finding a job in your chosen field once your studies are over. And while I do think it's important for dentists to be officially credentialed by the state (and airline pilots, and lawyers, and manicurists, for that matter), I am not convinced that we need officially credentialed novelists. History seems to agree with me on this point. Twelve North American writers have won the Nobel Prize in Literature since 1901: Not one of them had an MFA. Four of them never even got past high school.

These days, there are plenty of staggeringly expensive schools where you can go to study the arts. Some of them are fabulous; some of them, not so much. If you want to take that path, go for it—but know that it's an exchange, and make certain that this exchange truly benefits you. What the schools get from the exchange is clear: your money. What the students get out of the exchange depends on their devotion to learning, the seriousness of the program, and the quality of the teachers. To be sure, you can learn discipline in these programs, and style, and perhaps even courage. You may also meet your tribe at art school—those peers who will provide valuable professional connections and support for your ongoing career. You might even be lucky enough to find the mentor of your dreams, in the form of a particularly sensitive and engaged teacher. But I worry that what students of the arts are often seeking in higher education is nothing more than proof of their own legitimacy—proof that they are for real as creative people, because their degree says so.

On one hand, I completely understand this need for validation; it's an insecure pursuit, to attempt to create. But if you're working on your craft every day on your own, with steady discipline and love, then you are *already* for real as a creator, and you don't need to pay anybody to affirm that for you.

If you've already gone out and earned yourself an advanced degree in some creative field or another, no worries! If you're lucky, it made your art better, and at the very least I'm sure it did you no harm. Take whatever lessons you learned at school and use them to improve your craft. Or if you're getting a degree in the arts right now, and you can honestly and easily afford to do so, that's also fine. If your school gave you a free ride, better still. You're fortunate to be there, so use that good fortune to your advantage. Work hard, make the most of your opportunities, and grow, grow, grow. This can be a beautiful time of focused study and creative expansion. But if you're considering some sort of advanced schooling in the arts and you're not rolling in cash, I'm telling you—*you can live without it.* You can certainly live without the debt, because debt will always be the abattoir of creative dreams.

One of the best painters I know is a teacher at one of the world's most esteemed art schools—but my friend himself does not have an advanced degree. He is a master, yes, but he learned his mastery on his own. He became a great painter because he worked devilishly hard for years to become a great painter. Now he teaches others, at a level that he himself was never taught. Which kind of makes you question the necessity of the whole system. But students flock from all over the world to study at this school, and many of these students (the ones who are not from wealthy families, or who did not get a full ride of scholarships from the university) come out of that program with tens of thousands of dollars of debt. My friend cares immensely about his students, and so watching them fall so deeply into debt (while, paradoxically, they strive to become more like *him*) makes this good man feel sick in the heart, and it makes me feel sick in the heart, too.

When I asked my friend why they do it—why these students mortgage their futures so deeply for a few years of creative study—he said, "Well, the truth is, they don't always think it through. Most artists are impulsive people who don't plan very far ahead. Artists, by nature, are gamblers. Gambling is a dangerous habit. But whenever you make art, you're always gambling. You're rolling the dice on the slim odds that your investment of time, energy, and resources now might pay off later in a big way—that somebody might buy your work, and that you might become successful. Many of my students are gambling that their expensive education will be worth it in the long run."

I get this. I've always been creatively impulsive, too. It comes with the territory of curiosity and passion. I take leaps and gambles with my work all the time—or at least I try to. You must be willing to take risks if you want to live a creative existence. But if you're going to gamble, *know that you are gambling*. Never roll the dice without being aware that you are holding a pair of dice in your hands. And make certain that you can actually cover your bets (both emotionally and financially).

My fear is that many people pay through the nose for advanced schooling in the arts without realizing that they're actually gambling, because—on the surface—it can look like they're making a sound investment in their future. After all, isn't school where people go to learn a profession—and isn't a profession a responsible and respectable thing to acquire? But the arts are not a *profession*, in the manner of regular professions. There is no job security in creativity, and there never will be.

Going into massive debt in order to become a creator, then, can make a stress and a burden out of something that should only ever have been a joy and a release. And after having invested so much in their education, artists who don't immediately find professional success (which is most artists) can feel like failures. Their sense of having failed can interfere with their creative self-confidence—and maybe even stop them from creating at all. Then they're in the terrible position of having to deal not only with a sense of shame and failure, but also with steep monthly bills that will forever remind them of their shame and failure.

Please understand that I am not against higher education by any means; I am merely against crippling indebtedness—particularly for those who wish to live a creative life. And recently (at least here in America) the concept of higher education has become virtually synonymous with crippling indebtedness. Nobody needs debt less than an artist. So try not to fall into that trap. And if you have already fallen into that trap, try to claw your way out of it by any means necessary, as soon as you can. Free yourself so that you can live and create more freely, as you were designed by nature to do.

Be careful with yourself, is what I'm saying.

Be careful about safeguarding your future—but also about safeguarding your sanity.

Try This Instead

Instead of taking out loans to go to a school for the arts, maybe try to push yourself deeper into the world, to explore more bravely. Or go more deeply and bravely inward. Take an honest inventory of the education you *already* have—the years you have lived, the trials you have endured, the skills you have learned along the way.

If you are a young person, open your eyes wide and let the world educate you to the fullest extent. ("Ascend no longer from the textbook!" warned Walt Whitman, and I warn it, too; there are many ways to learn that do not necessarily involve schoolrooms.) And feel free to start sharing your perspective through creativity, even if you're just a kid. If you are young, you see things differently than I do, and I want to know how you see things. We all want to know. When we look at your work (whatever your work may be), we will want to feel your youth—that fresh sense of your recent arrival here. Be generous with us and let us feel it. After all, for many of us it has been so long since we stood where you now stand.

If you are older, trust that the world has been educating you all along. You already know so much more than you think you know. You are not finished; you are merely *ready*. After a certain age, no matter how you've been spending your time, you have very likely earned a doctorate in living. If you're still here—if you have survived this long—it is because you know things. We need you to reveal to us what you know, what you have learned, what you have seen and felt. If you are older, chances are strong that you may already possess absolutely everything you need to possess in order to live a more creative life—except the confidence to actually do your work. But we need you to do your work.

Whether you are young or old, we need your work in order to enrich and inform our own lives.

So take your insecurities and your fears and hold them upside down by their ankles and shake yourself free of all your cumbersome ideas about what you require (and how much you need to pay) in order to become creatively legitimate. Because I'm telling you that you are *already* creatively legitimate, by nature of your mere existence here among us.

Your Teachers

Do you want to study under the great teachers? Is that it?

Well, you can find them anywhere. They live on the shelves of your library; they live on the walls of museums; they live in recordings made decades ago. Your teachers don't even need to be alive to educate you masterfully. No living writer has ever taught me more about plotting and characterization than Charles Dickens has taught me—and needless to say, I never met with him during office hours to discuss it. All I had to do in order to learn from Dickens was to spend years privately studying his novels like they were holy scripture, and then to practice like the devil on my own.

Aspiring writers are lucky in a way, because writing is such a private (and cheap) affair and always has been. With other creative pursuits, admittedly it's trickier and can be far more costly. Strict, supervised training can be essential if you want to be, for instance, a professional opera singer, or a classical cellist. For centuries, people have studied at music conservatories, or dance or art academies. Many marvelous creators have emerged from such schools over time. Then again, many other marvelous creators did not.

And many talented people acquired all that magnificent education, but never put it into practice.

Most of all, there is this truth: No matter how great your teachers may be, and no matter how esteemed your academy's reputation, eventually you will have to do the work by yourself. Eventually, the teachers won't be there anymore. The walls of the school will fall away, and you'll be on your own. The hours that you will then put into practice, study, auditions, and creation will be entirely up to you.

The sooner and more passionately you get married to this idea—*that it is ultimately entirely up to you*—the better off you'll be.

The Fat Kids

Here's what I did during my twenties, rather than going to school for writing: I got a job as a waitress at a diner.

Later, I became a bartender, as well. I've also worked as an au pair, a private tutor, a ranch hand, a cook, a teacher, a flea-marketeer, and a bookstore clerk. I lived in cheap apartments, had no car, and wore thrift-shop clothes. I would work every shift, save all my money, and then go off traveling for a while to learn things. I wanted to meet people, and to hear their stories. Writers are told to write what they know, and all I knew was that I didn't know very much yet, so I went forth in deliberate search of material. Working at the diner was great, because I had access to dozens of different voices a day. I kept two notebooks in my back pockets—one for my customers' orders, and the other for my customers' dialogue. Working at the bar was even better, because those characters were often tipsy and thus were even more forthcoming with their narratives. (As a bartender, I learned that not only does everybody have a story that would stop your heart, but everybody wants to tell you about it.)

I sent my work out to publications, and I collected rejection letters in return. I kept up with my writing, despite the rejections. I labored over my short stories alone in my bedroom—and also in train stations, in stairwells, in libraries, in public parks, and in the apartments of various friends, boyfriends, and relatives. I sent more and more work out. I was rejected, rejected, rejected, rejected.

I disliked the rejection letters. Who wouldn't? But I took the long view: My intention was to spend my entire life in communion with writing, period. (And people in my family live forever—I have a grandmother who's one hundred and two!—so I figured my twenties was too soon to start panicking about time running out.) That being the case, editors could reject me all they wanted; I wasn't going anywhere. Whenever I got those rejection letters, then, I would permit my ego to say aloud to whoever had signed it: "You think you can scare me off? I've got another eighty years to wear you down! There are people who *haven't even been born yet* who are gonna reject me someday—that's how long I plan to stick around."

Then I would put the letter away and get back to work.

I decided to play the game of rejection letters as if it were a great cosmic tennis match: Somebody would send me a rejection, and I would knock it right back over the net, sending out another query that same afternoon. My policy was: *You hit it to me, I'm going to hit it straight back out into the universe.*

I had to do it this way, I knew, because nobody was going to put my work out there for me. I had no advocate, no agent, no patron, no connections. (Not only did I not know anyone who had a job in the publishing world, I barely knew anyone who had a *job*.) I knew that nobody was ever going to knock on my apartment door and say, "We understand that a very talented unpublished young writer lives here, and we would like to help her advance her career." No, I would have to announce myself, and so I did announce myself. Repeatedly. I remember having the distinct sense that I might never wear them down—those faceless, nameless guardians of the gate that I was tirelessly besieging. They might never give in to me. They might never let me in. It might never work.

It didn't matter.

No way was I going to give up on my work simply because it wasn't "working." That wasn't the point of it. The rewards could not come from the external results—I knew that. The rewards had to come from the joy of puzzling out the work itself, and from the private awareness I held that I had chosen a devotional path and I was being true to it. If someday I got lucky enough to be paid for my work, that would be great, but in the meantime, money could always come from other places. There are so many ways in this world to make a good enough living, and I tried lots of them, and I always got by well enough.

I was happy. I was a total nobody, and I was happy.

I saved my earnings and went on trips and took notes. I went to the pyramids of Mexico and took notes. I went on bus rides through the suburbs of New Jersey and took notes. I went to Eastern Europe and took notes. I went to parties and took notes. I went to Wyoming and worked as a trail cook on a ranch and took notes.

At some point in my twenties, I gathered together a few friends who also wanted to be writers, and we started our own workshop. We met twice a month for several years and we read one another's work loyally. For reasons that are lost to history, we named ourselves the Fat Kids. It was the world's most perfect literary workshop—or at least it was in our eyes. We had selected one another carefully, thereby precluding the killjoys and bullies who show up in many workshops to stomp on people's dreams. We held each other to deadlines and encouraged each other to submit our work to publishers. We came to know each other's voices and hang-ups, and we helped each other to work through our specific habitual obstacles. We ate pizza and we laughed.

The Fat Kids Workshop was productive and inspiring and fun. It was a safe place in which to be creative and vulnerable and exploratory—and it was completely and totally free. (Except for the pizza, yes, of course. But, come on! You see what I'm getting at, right? You can do this stuff *yourself*, people!)

Werner Herzog Chimes In

I have a friend in Italy who's an independent filmmaker. Many years ago, back when he was an angry young man, he wrote a letter to his hero, the great German director Werner Herzog. My friend poured out his heart in this letter, complaining to Herzog about how badly his career was going, how nobody liked his movies, how difficult it had become to make films in a world where nobody cares, where everything is so expensive, where there is no funding for the arts, where public tastes have run to the vulgar and the commercial . . .

If he'd been looking for sympathy, however, my friend had gone to the wrong place. (Although why anyone would turn to *Werner Herzog*, of all people, for a warm shoulder to cry on is beyond me.) Anyhow, Herzog wrote my friend a long reply of ferocious challenge, in which he said, more or less, this:

"Quit your complaining. It's not the world's fault that you wanted to be an artist. It's not the world's job to enjoy the films you make, and it's certainly not the world's obligation to pay for your dreams. Nobody wants to hear it. Steal a camera if you must, but stop whining and get back to work."

(In this story, I've just realized, Werner Herzog was essentially playing the role of my mother. How wonderful!)

My friend framed the letter and hung it over his desk, as well he should have. Because while Herzog's admonition might seem like a rebuke, it wasn't; it was an attempt at liberation. I think it's a mighty act of human love to remind somebody that they can accomplish things by themselves, and that the world does not automatically owe them any reward, and that they are not as weak and hobbled as they may believe.

Such reminders can seem blunt, and often we don't want to hear them, but there is a simple question of self-respect at play here. There is something magnificent about encouraging someone to step forward into his own self-respect at last—especially when it comes to creating something brave and new.

That letter, in other words?

It was my friend's permission slip.

He got back to work.

A Trick

So, yeah—here's a trick: Stop complaining.

Trust me on this. Trust Werner Herzog on this, too.

There are so many good reasons to stop complaining if you want to live a more creative life.

First of all, it's annoying. Every artist complains, so it's a dead and boring topic. (From the volume of complaints that emerges from the professional creative class, you would think these people had been sentenced to their vocations by an evil dictator, rather than having chosen their work with a free will and an open heart.)

Second, of *course* it's difficult to create things; if it wasn't difficult, everyone would be doing it, and it wouldn't be special or interesting.

Third, nobody ever really listens to anybody else's complaints, anyhow, because we're all too focused on our own holy struggle, so basically you're just talking to a brick wall.

Fourth, and most important, *you're scaring away inspiration.* Every time you express a complaint about how difficult and tiresome it is to be creative, inspiration takes another step away from you, offended. It's almost like inspiration puts up its hands and says, "Hey, sorry, buddy! I didn't realize my presence was such a drag. I'll take my business elsewhere."

I have felt this phenomenon in my own life, whenever I start complaining. I have felt the way my self-pity slams the door on inspiration, making the room feel suddenly cold, small, and empty. That being the case, I took this path as a young person: I started telling myself that *I enjoyed my work.* I proclaimed that I enjoyed every single aspect of my creative endeavors—the agony and the ecstasy, the success and the failure, the joy and the embarrassment, the dry spells and the grind and the stumble and the confusion and the stupidity of it all.

I even dared to say this aloud.

I told the universe (and anyone who would listen) that I was committed to living a creative life not in order to save the world, not as an act of protest, not to become famous, not to gain entrance to the canon, not to challenge the system, not to show the bastards, not to prove to my family that I was worthy, not as a form of deep therapeutic emotional catharsis . . . but simply because *I liked it.*

So try saying this: "I enjoy my creativity."

And when you say it, be sure to actually mean it.

For one thing, it will freak people out. I believe that enjoying your work with all your heart is the only truly subversive position left to take as a creative person these days. It's such a gangster move, because hardly anybody ever dares to speak of creative enjoyment aloud, for fear of not being taken seriously as an artist. So say it. Be the weirdo who dares to enjoy.

Best of all, though, by saying that you delight in your work, you will draw inspiration near. Inspiration will be grateful to hear those words coming out of your mouth, because inspiration—like all of us—appreciates being appreciated. Inspiration will overhear your pleasure, and it will send ideas to your door as a reward for your enthusiasm and your loyalty.

More ideas than you could ever use.

Enough ideas for ten lifetimes.

Pigeonholing

Somebody said to me the other day, "You claim that we can all be creative, but aren't there huge differences between people's innate talents and abilities? Sure, we can all make some kind of art, but only a few of us can be *great*, right?"

I don't know.

Honestly, you guys, I don't even really care.

I cannot even be bothered to think about the difference between high art and low art. I will fall asleep with my face in my dinner plate if someone starts discoursing to me about the academic distinction between true mastery and mere craft. I certainly don't ever want to confidently announce that this person is destined to become an important artist, while that person should give it up.

How do I know? How does anyone know? It's all so wildly subjective, and, anyhow, life has surprised me too many times in this realm. On one hand, I've known brilliant people who created absolutely nothing from their talents. On the other hand, there are people whom I once arrogantly dismissed who later staggered me with the gravity and beauty of their work. It has all humbled me far beyond the ability to judge anyone's potential, or to rule anybody out.

I beg you not to worry about such definitions and distinctions, then, okay? It will only weigh you down and trouble your mind, and we need you to stay as light and unburdened as possible in order to keep you creating. Whether you think you're brilliant or you think you're a loser, just make whatever you need to make and toss it out there. Let other people pigeonhole you however they need to. And pigeonhole you they shall, because that's what people like to do. Actually, pigeonholing is something people *need* to do in order to feel that they have set the chaos of existence into some kind of reassuring order.

Thus, people will stick you into all sorts of boxes. They'll call you a genius, or a fraud, or an amateur, or a pretender, or a wannabe, or a has-been, or a hobbyist, or an also-ran, or a rising star, or a master of reinvention. They may say flattering things about you, or they may say dismissive things about you. They may call you a mere genre novelist, or a mere children's book illustrator, or a mere commercial photographer, or a mere community theater actor, or a mere home cook, or a mere weekend musician, or a mere crafter, or a mere landscape painter, or a mere whatever.

It doesn't matter in the least. Let people have their opinions. More than that—let people be in *love* with their opinions, just as you and I are in love with ours. But never delude yourself into believing that you require someone else's blessing (or even their comprehension) in order to make your own creative work. And always remember that people's judgments about you are none of your business.

Lastly, remember what W. C. Fields had to say on this point: "It ain't what they call you; it's what you answer to."

Actually, don't even bother answering.

Just keep doing your thing.

Fun House Mirrors

I once wrote a book that accidentally became a giant best seller, and for a few years there, it was like I was living in a hall of fun house mirrors.

It was never my intention to write a giant best seller, believe me. I wouldn't know how to write a giant best seller if I tried. (Case in point: I've published six books—all written with equal passion and effort—and five of them were decidedly *not* giant best sellers.)

I certainly did not feel, as I was writing *Eat Pray Love*, that I was producing the greatest or most important work of my life. I knew only that it was a departure for me to write something so personal, and I figured people might mock it for being so terribly earnest. But I wrote that book anyhow, because I needed to write it for my own intimate purposes—and also because I was curious to see if I could convey my emotional experiences adequately on paper. It never occurred to me that my own thoughts and feelings might intersect so intensely with the thoughts and feelings of so many other people.

I'll tell you how oblivious I was during the writing of that book. During the course of my *Eat Pray Love* travels,

I fell in love with that Brazilian man named Felipe, to whom I am now married, and at one point—shortly into our courtship—I asked him if he felt comfortable with my writing about him in my memoir. He said, "Well, it depends. What's at stake?"

I replied, "Nothing. Trust me—*nobody* reads my books."

Over twelve million people ended up reading that book.

And because so many people read it, and because so many people disagreed over it, somewhere along the way *Eat Pray Love* stopped being a book, per se, and it became something else—a huge screen upon which millions of people projected their most intense emotions. These emotions ranged from absolute hatred to blind adulation. I got letters saying, *I detest everything about you*, and I got letters saying, *You have written my bible.*

Imagine if I'd tried to create a definition of myself based on any of these reactions. I didn't try. And that's the only reason *Eat Pray Love* didn't throw me off my path as a writer—because of my deep and lifelong conviction that the results of my work don't have much to do with me. I can only be in charge of producing the work itself. That's a hard enough job. I refuse to take on additional jobs, such as trying to police what anybody thinks about my work once it leaves my desk.

Also, I realized that it would be unreasonable and

immature of me to expect that I should be allowed to have a voice of expression, but other people should not. If I am allowed to speak my inner truth, then my critics are allowed to speak their inner truths, as well. Fair's fair. If you dare to create something and put it out there, after all, then it may accidentally stir up a response. That's the natural order of life: the eternal inhale and exhale of action and reaction. But you are definitely not in charge of the reaction—even when that reaction is flat-out bizarre.

One day, for instance, a woman came up to me at a book signing and said, "*Eat Pray Love* changed my life. You inspired me to leave my abusive marriage and set myself free. It was all because of that one moment in your book—that moment when you describe putting a restraining order on your ex-husband because you'd had enough of his violence and you weren't going to tolerate it anymore."

A restraining order? Violence?

That never happened! Not in my book, nor in my actual life! You can't even read that narrative between the lines of my memoir, because it's so far from the truth. But that woman had subconsciously inserted that story—her own story—into my memoir, because, I suppose, she needed to. (It may have been easier for her, somehow, to believe that her burst of resolve and strength had come from me and not from herself.) Whatever her emotional motive, though, she had embroidered herself into my story and erased my actual narrative in the process. Strange as it seems, I submit that it was her absolute right to do this. I submit that this woman has the God-given right to misread my book however she wants to misread it. Once my book entered her hands, after all, everything about it belonged to her, and never again to me.

Recognizing this reality—that the reaction doesn't belong to you—is the only sane way to create. If people enjoy what you've created, terrific. If people ignore what you've created, too bad. If people misunderstand what you've created, don't sweat it. And what if people absolutely hate what you've created? What if people attack you with savage vitriol, and insult your intelligence, and malign your motives, and drag your good name through the mud?

Just smile sweetly and suggest—as politely as you possibly can—that they go make their own fucking art.

Then stubbornly continue making yours.

We Were Just a Band

Because, in the end, it really doesn't matter that much.

Because, in the end, *it's just creativity.*

Or, as John Lennon once said about the Beatles, "We were just a band!"

Please don't get me wrong: I adore creativity. (And of course I revere the Beatles.) I have dedicated my entire life to the pursuit of creativity, and I spend a lot of time encouraging other people to do the same, because I think a creative life is the most marvelous life there is.

Yes, some of my most transcendent moments have been during episodes of inspiration, or when I'm experiencing the magnificent creations of others. And, yes, I absolutely do believe that our artistic instincts have divine and magical origins, but that doesn't mean we have to take it all so seriously, because—in the final analysis—I still perceive that human artistic expression is blessedly, refreshingly nonessential.

That's exactly why I love it so much.

Radiation Canaries

Do you think I'm wrong? Are you one of those people who believe that the arts are the most serious and important thing in the world?

If so, my friend, then you and I must part ways right here.

I offer up my own life as irrefutable evidence that the arts don't matter as much as we sometimes trick ourselves into believing they do. Because let's be honest: You would be hard-pressed to identify a job that is not objectively more valuable to society than mine. Name a profession, any profession: teacher, doctor, fireman, custodian, roofer, rancher, security guard, political lobbyist, sex worker, even the ever-meaningless "consultant"—each is infinitely more essential to the smooth maintenance of the human community than any novelist ever was, or ever will be.

There was once a terrific exchange on the TV show *30 Rock* that distilled this idea down to its irreducible nucleus. Jack Donaghy was mocking Liz Lemon for her utter uselessness to society as a mere writer, while she tried to defend her fundamental social importance.

Jack: "In a postapocalyptic world, how would society even use you?"

Liz: "Traveling bard!"

Jack, in disgust: "Radiation canary."

I think Jack Donaghy was right, but I do not find this truth to be dispiriting. On the contrary, I find it thrilling. The fact that I get to spend my life making objectively useless things means that I *don't* live in a postapocalyptic dystopia. It means I am not exclusively chained to the grind of mere survival. It means we still have enough space left in our civilization for the luxuries of imagination and beauty and emotion—and even total frivolousness.

Pure creativity is magnificent expressly *because* it is the opposite of everything else in life that's essential or inescapable (food, shelter, medicine, rule of law, social order, community and familial responsibility, sickness, loss, death, taxes, etc.). Pure creativity is something better than a necessity; it's a gift. It's the frosting. Our creativity is a wild and unexpected bonus from the universe. It's as if all our gods and angels gathered together and said, "It's tough down there as a human being, we know. Here—have some delights."

It doesn't discourage me in the least, in other words, to know that my life's work is arguably useless.

All it does is make me want to *play*.

High Stakes vs. Low Stakes

Of course, it must be said there are dark and evil places in the world where people's creativity cannot simply stem from a sense of play and where personal expression has huge and serious repercussions.

If you happen to be a dissident journalist suffering in jail in Nigeria, or a radical filmmaker under house arrest in Iran, or an oppressed young female poet struggling to be heard in Afghanistan, or pretty much anybody in North Korea, then it *is* the case that your creative expression comes with extreme life-or-death stakes. There are people out there who bravely and stubbornly continue to make art despite living under god-awful totalitarian regimes, and those people are heroes, and we should all bow down to them.

But let's be honest with ourselves here: That ain't most of us.

In the safe world in which you and I most likely live, the stakes of our creative expression are *low.* Almost comically low. For instance: If a publisher dislikes my book, they may not publish my book, and that will make me sad, but nobody's going to come to my home and shoot me over it. Likewise, nobody ever died because I got a bad review in the *New York Times.* The polar ice caps will not melt any faster or slower because I couldn't figure out how to write a convincing ending to my novel.

Maybe I won't always be successful at my creativity, but the world won't end because of that. Maybe I won't always be able to make a living out of my writing, but that's not the end of the world, either, because there are lots of other ways to make a living besides writing books—and many of them are easier than writing books. And while it's definitely true that failure and criticism may bruise my precious ego, the fate of nations does not depend upon my precious ego. (Thank God.)

So let's try to wrap our minds around this reality: There's probably never going to be any such thing in your life or mine as "an arts emergency."

That being the case, why not make art?

Tom Waits Chimes In

Years ago, I interviewed the musician Tom Waits for a profile in *GQ* magazine. I've spoken about this interview before and I will probably speak about it forever, because I've never met anyone who was so articulate and wise about creative living.

In the course of our interview, Waits went on a whimsical rant about all the different forms that song ideas will take when they're trying to be born. Some songs, he said, will come to him with an almost absurd ease, "like dreams taken through a straw." Other songs, though, he has to work hard for, "like digging potatoes out of the ground." Still other songs are sticky and weird, "like gum found under an old table," while some songs are like wild birds that he must come at sideways, sneaking up on them gently so as not to scare them into flight.

The most difficult and petulant songs, though, will only respond to a firm hand and an authoritative voice. There are songs, Waits says, that simply will not allow themselves to be born, and that will hold up the recording of an entire album. Waits has, at such moments, cleared the studio of all the other musicians and technicians so he can have a stern talking-to with a particularly obstinate song. He'll pace the studio alone, saying aloud, "Listen, you! We're all going for a ride together! The whole family's already in the van! You have five minutes to get on board, or else this album is leaving without you!"

Sometimes it works.

Sometimes it doesn't.

Sometimes you have to let it go. Some songs just aren't serious about wanting to be born yet, Waits said. They only want to annoy you, and waste your time, and hog your attention—perhaps while they're waiting for a different artist to come along. He has become philosophical about such things. He used to suffer and anguish over losing songs, he said, but now he *trusts.* If a song is serious about being born, he trusts that it will come to him in the right manner, at the right time. If not, he will send it along its way, with no hard feelings.

"Go bother someone else," he'll tell the annoying song-that-doesn't-want-to-be-a-song. "Go bother Leonard Cohen."

Over the years, Tom Waits finally found his sense of permission to deal with his creativity more lightly—without so much drama, without so much fear. A lot of this lightness, Waits said, came from watching his children grow up and seeing their total freedom of creative expression. He noticed that his children felt fully entitled to make up songs all the time, and when they were done with them, they would toss them out "like little origami things, or paper airplanes." Then they would sing the next song that came through the channel. They never seemed to worry that the flow of ideas would dry up. They never stressed about their creativity, and they never competed against themselves; they merely lived within their inspiration, comfortably and unquestioningly.

Waits had once been the opposite of that as a creator. He told me that he'd struggled deeply with his creativity in his youth because—like many serious young men—he wanted to be regarded as important, meaningful, heavy. He wanted his work to be better than other people's work. He wanted to be complex and intense. There was anguish, there was torment, there was drinking, there were dark nights of the soul. He was lost in the cult of artistic suffering, but he called that suffering by another name: dedication.

But through watching his children create so freely, Waits had an epiphany: It wasn't actually that big a deal. He told me, "I realized that, as a songwriter, the only thing I really do is make jewelry for the inside of other people's minds." Music is nothing more than decoration for the imagination. That's all it is. That realization, Waits said, seemed to open things up for him. Songwriting became less painful after that.

Intracranial jewelry-making! What a cool job!

That's basically what we all do—all of us who spend our days making and doing interesting things for no particularly rational reason. As a creator, you can design any sort of jewelry that you like for the inside of other people's minds (or simply for the inside of your own mind). You can make work that's provocative, aggressive, sacred, edgy, traditional, earnest, devastating, entertaining, brutal, fanciful . . . but when all is said and done, it's still just intracranial jewelry-making. It's still just decoration. And that's glorious. But it's seriously not something that anybody needs to hurt themselves over, okay?

So relax a bit, is what I'm saying.

Please try to relax.

Otherwise, what's the point of having all these wonderful senses in the first place?

The Central Paradox

In conclusion, then, art is absolutely meaningless.

It is, however, also deeply meaningful.

That's a paradox, of course, but we're all adults here, and

I think we can handle it. I think we can all hold two mutually contradictory ideas at the same time without our heads exploding. So let's give this one a try. The paradox that you need to comfortably inhabit, if you wish to live a contented creative life, goes something like this: "My creative expression must be the most important thing in the world to me (if I am to live artistically), and it also must not matter at all (if I am to live sanely)."

Sometimes you will need to leap from one end of this paradoxical spectrum to the other in a matter of minutes, and then back again. As I write this book, for instance, I approach each sentence as if the future of humanity depends upon my getting that sentence just right. I care, because I want it to be lovely. Therefore, anything less than a full commitment to that sentence is lazy and dishonorable. But as I edit my sentence—sometimes immediately after writing it—I have to be willing to throw it to the dogs and never look back. (Unless, of course, I decide that I need that sentence again after all, in which case I must dig up its bones, bring it back to life, and once again regard it as sacred.)

It matters./It doesn't matter.

Build space in your head for this paradox. Build as much space for it as you can.

Build even more space.

You will need it.

And then go deep within that space—as far in as you can possibly go—and make absolutely whatever you want to make.

It's nobody's business but your own.

Persistence

Taking Vows

When I was about sixteen years old, I took vows to become a writer.

I mean, I *literally* took vows—the way a young woman of an entirely different nature might take vows to become a nun. Of course, I had to invent my own ceremony around these vows, because there is no official holy Sacrament for a teenager who longs to become a writer, but I used my imagination and my passion and I made it happen. I retreated to my bedroom one night and turned off all the lights. I lit a candle, got down on my honest-to-God knees, and swore my fidelity to writing for the rest of my natural life.

My vows were strangely specific and, I would still argue, pretty realistic. I didn't make a promise that I would be a successful writer, because I sensed that success was not under my control. Nor did I promise that I would be a great writer, because I didn't know if I could be great. Nor did I give myself any time limits for the work, like, "If I'm not published by the time I'm thirty, I'll give up on this dream and go find another line of work." In fact, I didn't put any conditions or restrictions on my path at all. My deadline was: never.

Instead, I simply vowed to the universe that I would write forever, regardless of the result. I promised that I would try to be brave about it, and grateful, and as uncomplaining as I could possibly be. I also promised that I would never ask writing to take care of me financially, but that *I would always take care of it*—meaning that I would always support us both, by any means necessary. I did not ask for any external rewards for my devotion; I just wanted to spend my life as near to writing as possible—forever close to that source of all my curiosity and contentment—and so I was willing to make whatever arrangements needed to be made in order to get by.

Learning

The curious thing is, I actually kept those vows. I kept them for years. I still keep them. I have broken many promises in my life (including a marriage vow), but I have never broken that promise.

I even kept those vows through the chaos of my twenties—a time in my life when I was shamefully irresponsible in every other imaginable way. Yet despite all my immaturity and carelessness and recklessness, I still honored my vows to writing with the fealty of a holy pilgrim.

I wrote every day throughout my twenties. For a while, I had a boyfriend who was a musician, and he practiced every day. He played scales; I wrote small fictional scenes. It was the same idea—to keep your hand in your craft, to stay close to it. On bad days, when I felt no inspiration at all, I would set the kitchen timer for thirty minutes and make myself sit there and scribble something, *anything*. I had read an interview with John Updike where he said that some of the best novels you've ever read were written in an hour a day; I figured I could always carve out at least thirty minutes somewhere to dedicate myself to my work, no matter what else was going on or how badly I believed the work was going.

Generally speaking, the work did go badly, too. I *really* didn't know what I was doing. I felt sometimes like I was trying to carve scrimshaw while wearing oven mitts. Everything took forever. I had no chops, no game. It could take me a whole year just to finish one tiny short story. Most of the time, all I was doing was imitating my favorite authors, anyhow. I went through a Hemingway stage (who doesn't?), but I also went through a pretty serious Annie Proulx stage and a rather embarrassing Cormac McCarthy stage. But that's what you have to do at the beginning; everybody imitates before they can innovate.

For a while, I tried to write like a Southern gothic novelist, because I found that to be a far more exotic voice than my own New England sensibility. I was not an especially convincing Southern writer, of course, but that's only because I'd never lived a day in the South. (A friend of mine who actually was from the South said to me in exasperation, after reading one of my stories, "You've got all these old men sittin' around the porch eatin' peanuts, and you ain't never sat around a porch eatin' peanuts in your *life*! You got some nerve, girl!" Oh, well. We try.)

None of it was easy, but that wasn't the point. I had

never asked writing to be easy; I had only asked writing to be *interesting*. And it was always interesting to me. Even when I couldn't do it right, it was still interesting to me. It still interests me. Nothing has ever interested me more. That profound sense of interest kept me working, even as I had no tangible successes.

And slowly I improved.

It's a simple and generous rule of life that whatever you practice, you will improve at. For instance: If I had spent my twenties playing basketball every single day, or making pastry dough every single day, or studying auto mechanics every single day, I'd probably be pretty good at foul shots and croissants and transmissions by now.

Instead, I learned how to write.

A Caveat

But this does not mean that unless you began your creative endeavors in your twenties, it's too late!

God, no! Please don't get that idea.

It's never too late.

I could give you dozens of examples of amazing people

who didn't start following their creative paths until later—sometimes much later—in life. But for the sake of economy, I will only tell you about one of them.

Her name was Winifred.

I knew Winifred back in the 1990s, in Greenwich Village. I first met her at her ninetieth birthday party, which was quite a wild bash. She was a friend of a friend of mine (a guy who was in his twenties; Winifred had friends of all ages and backgrounds). Winifred was a bit of a luminary around Washington Square back in the day. She was a full-on bohemian legend who had lived in the Village forever. She had long red hair that she wore piled glamorously on top of her head, she was always draped in ropes of amber beads, and she and her late husband (a scientist) had spent their vacations chasing typhoons and hurricanes all over the world, just for fun. She kind of *was* a hurricane herself.

Winifred was the most vividly alive woman I had ever met in my young life, so one day, looking for inspiration, I asked her, "What's the best book you've ever read?"

She said, "Oh, darling. I could never narrow it down to just one book, because so many books are important to me. But I can tell you my favorite *subject.* Ten years ago, I began studying the history of ancient Mesopotamia, and it became my passion, and let me tell you—*it has totally changed my life.*"

For me, at the age of twenty-five, to hear a ninety-year-old widow speak of having her life changed by passion (and so recently!) was a revelation. It was one of those moments where I could almost *feel* my perspective expanding, as if my mind were being ratcheted open several notches and was now welcoming in all sorts of new possibilities for what a woman's life could look like.

But as I learned more about Winifred's passion, what struck me most was that she was now an acknowledged expert in the history of ancient Mesopotamia. She had given that field of study an entire decade of her life, after all—and if you devote yourself to *anything* diligently for ten years, that will make you an expert. (That's the time it would take to earn two master's degrees and a doctorate.) She had gone to the Middle East on several archaeological digs; she had learned cuneiform script; she was friendly with the greatest scholars and curators on the subject; she had never missed a related museum exhibit or lecture when it came to town. People now sought out Winifred for answers about ancient Mesopotamia, because now *she* was the authority.

I was a young woman who had only recently finished college. There was still some dull and limited part of my imagination that believed my education was over because NYU had granted me a diploma. Meeting Winifred, though, made me realize that your education isn't over when *they* say it's over; your education is over when *you* say it's over. And Winifred—back when she was a mere girl of eighty—had firmly decided: *It ain't over yet.*

So when can you start pursuing your most creative and passionate life?

You can start whenever you decide to start.

The Empty Bucket

I kept working.

I kept writing.

I kept not getting published, but that was okay, because I was getting *educated.*

The most important benefit of my years of disciplined, solitary work was that I began to recognize the emotional patterns of creativity—or, rather, I began to recognize *my* patterns. I could see that there were psychological cycles to my own creative process, and that those cycles were always pretty much the same.

"Ah," I learned to say when I would inevitably begin to lose heart for a project just a few weeks after I'd enthusiastically begun it. "This is the part of the process where I wish I'd never engaged with this idea at all. I remember this. I always go through this stage."

Or: "This is the part where I tell myself that I'll never write a good sentence again."

Or: "This is the part where I beat myself up for being a lazy loser."

Or: "This is the part where I begin fantasizing in terror about how bad the reviews are going to be—if this thing even gets published at all."

Or, once the project was finished: "This is the part where I panic that I'll never be able to make anything again."

Over years of devotional work, though, I found that if I just stayed with the process and didn't panic, I could pass safely through each stage of anxiety and on to the next level. I heartened myself with reminders that these fears were completely natural human reactions to interaction with the unknown. If I could convince myself that I was supposed to be there—that we are *meant* to engage with inspiration, and that inspiration *wants* to work with us—then I could usually get through my emotional minefield without blowing myself up before the project was finished.

At such times, I could almost hear creativity talking to me while I spun off into fear and doubt.

Stay with me, it would say. *Come back to me. Trust me.*

I decided to trust it.

My single greatest expression of stubborn gladness has been the endurance of that trust.

A particularly elegant commentary on this instinct came from the Nobel laureate Seamus Heaney, who said that—when one is learning how to write poetry—one should not expect it to be immediately good. The aspiring poet is constantly lowering a bucket only halfway down a well, coming up time and again with nothing but empty air. The frustration is immense. But you must keep doing it, anyway.

After many years of practice, Heaney explained, "the chain draws unexpectedly tight and you have dipped into waters that will continue to entice you back. You'll have broken the skin on the pool of yourself."

The Shit Sandwich

Back in my early twenties, I had a good friend who was an aspiring writer, just like me. I remember how he used to descend into dark funks of depression about his lack of success, about his inability to get published. He would sulk and rage.

"I don't want to be sitting around," he would moan. "I want this to all add up to something. I want this to become my *job*!"

Even back then, I thought there was something off about his attitude.

Mind you, I wasn't being published, either, and I was hungry, too. I would've *loved* to have all the same stuff he wanted—success, reward, affirmation. I was no stranger to disappointment and frustration. But I remember thinking that learning how to endure your disappointment and frustration *is* part of the job of a creative person. If you want to be an artist of any sort, it seemed to me, then handling your frustration is a fundamental aspect of the work—perhaps the single most fundamental aspect of the work. Frustration is not an interruption of your process; frustration *is* the process. The fun part (the part where it doesn't feel like work at all) is when you're actually creating something wonderful, and everything's going great, and everyone loves it, and you're flying high. But such instants are rare. You don't just get to leap from bright moment to bright moment. How you manage yourself *between* those bright moments, when things aren't going so great, is a measure of how devoted you are to your vocation, and how equipped you are for the weird demands of creative living. Holding yourself together through all the phases of creation is where the real work lies.

I recently read a fabulous blog by a writer named Mark Manson, who said that the secret to finding your purpose in life is to answer this question in total honesty: "What's your favorite flavor of shit sandwich?"

What Manson means is that every single pursuit—no matter how wonderful and exciting and glamorous it may initially seem—comes with its own brand of shit sandwich, its own lousy side effects. As Manson writes with profound wisdom: "Everything sucks, some of the time." You just have to decide what sort of suckage you're willing to deal with. So the question is not so much "What are you passionate about?" The question is "What are you passionate *enough* about that you can endure the most disagreeable aspects of the work?"

Manson explains it this way: "If you want to be a professional artist, but you aren't willing to see your work rejected hundreds, if not thousands, of times, then you're done before you start. If you want to be a hotshot court lawyer, but can't stand the eighty-hour workweeks, then I've got bad news for you."

Because if you love and want something enough—whatever it is—then you don't really mind eating the shit sandwich that comes with it.

If you truly love having babies, for instance, then you don't care about the morning sickness.

If you truly want to be a minister, you don't mind listening to other people's problems.

If you truly love performing, you will accept the discomforts and inconveniences of living on the road.

If you truly want to see the world, you'll risk getting pickpocketed on a train.

If you truly want to practice your figure skating, you'll get up before dawn on cold mornings to go to the ice rink and skate.

My friend back in the day claimed that he wanted to be a writer with all his heart, but it turns out he didn't want to eat the shit sandwich that comes along with that pursuit. He loved writing, sure, but he didn't love it *enough* to endure the ignominy of not getting the results he wanted, when he wanted them. He didn't want to work so hard at anything unless he was guaranteed some measure of worldly success on his own terms.

Which means, I think, that he only wanted to be a writer with *half* his heart.

And yeah, soon enough, he quit.

Which left me hungrily eyeballing his half-eaten shit sandwich, wanting to ask, "Are you gonna finish that?"

Because that's how much I loved the work: I would even eat *somebody else's shit sandwich* if it meant that I got to spend more time writing.

Your Day Job

The whole time I was practicing to be a writer, I always had a day job.

Even after I got published, I didn't quit my day job, just to be on the safe side. In fact, I didn't quit my day job (or my day *jobs*, I should say) until I had already written three books—and those three books were all published by major houses and were all reviewed nicely in the *New York Times*. One of them had even been nominated for a National Book Award. From an outside perspective, it might have looked like I'd already made it. But I wasn't taking any chances, so I kept my day job.

It wasn't until my fourth book (and that book was freaking *Eat Pray Love*, for heaven's sake) that I finally allowed myself to quit all other work and become nothing other than a writer of books.

I held on to those other sources of income for so long because I never wanted to burden my writing with the responsibility of paying for my life. I knew better than to ask this of my writing, because over the years, I have watched so many other people murder their creativity by demanding that their art pay the bills. I've seen artists drive themselves broke and crazy because of this insistence that they are not legitimate creators unless they can exclusively live off their creativity. And when their creativity fails them (meaning: doesn't pay the rent), they descend into resentment, anxiety, or even bankruptcy. Worst of all, they often quit creating at all.

I've always felt like this is so cruel to your work—to demand a regular paycheck from it, as if creativity were a government job, or a trust fund. Look, if you can manage to live comfortably off your inspiration forever, that's fantastic. That's everyone's dream, right? But don't let that dream turn into a nightmare. Financial demands can put so much pressure on the delicacies and vagaries of inspiration. You must be smart about providing for yourself. To claim that you are too creative to think about financial questions is to infantilize yourself—and I beg you not to infantilize yourself, because it's demeaning to your soul. (While it's lovely to be child*like* in your pursuit of creativity, in other words, it's dangerous to be child*ish*.)

Other self-infantilizing fantasies include: the dream of marrying for money, the dream of inheriting money, the dream of winning the lottery, and the dream of finding a "studio wife" (male or female) who will look after all your mundane concerns so that you can be free to commune with inspiration forever in a peaceful cocoon, utterly sheltered from the inconveniences of reality.

Come, now.

This is a *world*, not a womb. You can look after yourself in this world while looking after your creativity at the same time—just as people have done for ages. What's more, there is a profound sense of honor to be found in looking after yourself, and that honor will resonate powerfully in your work; it will make your work *stronger.*

Also, it may be the case that there are seasons when you can live off your art and seasons when you cannot. This need not be regarded as a crisis; it's only natural in the flux and uncertainty of a creative life. Or maybe you took a big risk in order to follow some creative dream and it didn't quite pay off, so now you have to work for the man for a while to save up money until it's time to go chase your next dream—that's fine, too. Just do it. But to yell at your creativity, saying, "You must earn money for me!" is sort of like yelling at a cat; it has no idea what you're talking about, and all you're doing is scaring it away, because you're making really loud noises and your face looks weird when you do that.

I held on to my day jobs for so long because I wanted to

keep my creativity free and safe. I maintained alternative streams of income so that, when my inspiration wasn't flowing, I could say to it reassuringly, "No worries, mate. Just take your time. I'm here whenever you're ready." I was always willing to work hard so that my creativity could play lightly. In so doing, I became my *own* patron; I became my *own* studio wife.

So many times I have longed to say to stressed-out, financially strapped artists, "Just take the pressure off yourself, dude, and get a job!"

There's no dishonor in having a job. What is dishonorable is scaring away your creativity by demanding that it pay for your entire existence. This is why, whenever anyone tells me they're quitting their day job in order to write a novel, my palms get a little sweaty. This is why, when anyone tells me that their plan for getting out of debt is to sell their first screenplay, I'm like, *Yikes.*

Write that novel, yes! Definitely try to sell that screenplay! I hope with all my heart that good fortune finds you and showers you with abundance. But don't count on the payoff, I beg of you—only because such payoffs are exceedingly rare, and you might very well kill off your creativity by holding it to such a harsh ultimatum.

You can always make your art on the side of your bread-

and-butter job. That's what I did for three whole books—and if it hadn't been for the bananas success of *Eat Pray Love*, that's what I'd still be doing now. That's what Toni Morrison did when she used to get up at five o'clock in the morning in order to work on her novels before going off to her real-life career in the publishing world. That's what J. K. Rowling did back when she was an impoverished single mother, struggling to get by and writing on the side. That's what my friend Ann Patchett did back when she worked as a waitress at TGI Fridays and wrote in her spare hours. That's what a busy married couple I know does—both of them illustrators, both of them with full-time jobs—when, every morning, they rise a full hour before their children awake to sit across from each other in their small studio space and quietly draw.

People don't do this kind of thing because they have all kinds of extra time and energy for it; they do this kind of thing because their creativity matters to them enough that they are willing to make all kinds of extra sacrifices for it.

Unless you come from landed gentry, that's what *everyone* does.

Paint Your Ox

For most of human history, then, the vast majority of people have made their art in stolen moments, using scraps of borrowed time—and often using pilfered or discarded materials, to boot. (The Irish poet Patrick Kavanagh says it marvelously: "See over there / A created splendour / Made by one individual / From things residual.")

I once encountered a man in India who owned nothing of value but an ox. The ox had two handsome horns. In order to celebrate his ox, the man had painted one of the horns hot pink and the other turquoise blue. He then glued little bells to the tips of each horn, so that when the ox shook its head, its flashy pink and blue horns made a cheerful tinkling sound.

This hardworking and financially stressed man had only one valuable possession, but he had embellished it to the max, using whatever materials he could get his hands on—a bit of house paint, a touch of glue, and some bells. As a result of his creativity, he now possessed the most interesting-looking ox in town. For what? Just *because.* Because a decorated ox is better than a non-decorated ox, obviously! (As evidenced by the fact that—eleven years later—the only animal I can still distinctly remember from my visit to that small Indian village is that fantastically decked-out ox.)

Is this the ideal environment in which to create—having to make art out of "things residual" in stolen time? Not really. Or maybe it's *fine.* Maybe it doesn't matter, because that's how things have always been made. Most individuals have never had enough time, and they've never had enough resources, and they've never had enough support or patronage or reward . . . and yet still they persist in creating. They persist because they care. They persist because they are called to be makers, by any means necessary.

Money helps, to be sure. But if money were the only thing people needed in order to live creative lives, then the mega-rich would be the most imaginative, generative, and original thinkers among us, and they simply are not. The essential ingredients for creativity remain exactly the same for everybody: courage, enchantment, permission, persistence, trust—and those elements are universally accessible. Which does not mean that creative living is always easy; it merely means that creative living is always *possible.*

I once read a heartbreaking letter that Herman Melville wrote to his good friend Nathaniel Hawthorne, complaining that he simply could not find time to work on his book about that whale, because "I am so pulled hither and thither by circumstances." Melville said that he longed for a big, wide-open stretch of time in which to create (he called it "the calm, the coolness, the silent grass-growing mood in which a man *ought* always to compose"), but that sort of luxuriousness simply did not exist for him. He was broke, he was stressed, and he could not find the hours to write in peace.

I do not know of any artist (successful or unsuccessful, amateur or pro) who does not long for that kind of time. I do not know of any creative soul who does not dream of calm, cool, grass-growing days in which to work without interruption. Somehow, though, nobody ever seems to achieve it. Or if they do achieve it (through a grant, for instance, or a friend's generosity, or an artist's residency), that idyll is just temporary—and then life will inevitably rush back in. Even the most successful creative people I know complain that they never seem to get *all* the hours they need in order to engage in dreamy, pressure-free, creative exploration. Reality's demands are constantly pounding on the door and disturbing them. On some other planet, in some other lifetime, perhaps that sort of peaceful Edenic work environment does exist, but it rarely exists here on earth.

Melville never got that kind of environment, for instance.

But he still somehow managed to write *Moby-Dick*, anyhow.

Have an Affair

Why do people persist in creating, even when it's difficult and inconvenient and often financially unrewarding?

They persist because they are in love.

They persist because they are hot for their vocation.

Let me explain what I mean by *hot.*

You know how people who are having extramarital affairs always seem to manage to find time to see each other in order to have wild, transgressive sex? It doesn't seem to matter if those people have full-time jobs and families at home to support; they still somehow always manage to find the time to sneak off and see their lover—no matter what the difficulties, the risks, or the costs. Even if they get only fifteen minutes together in a stairwell, they will take that time and they will make out with each other like crazy. (If anything, the fact that they have only fifteen minutes together somehow makes it all even hotter.)

When people are having an affair, they don't mind losing sleep, or missing meals. They will make whatever sacrifices they have to make, and they will blast through any obstacles, in order to be alone with the object of their devotion and obsession—*because it matters to them.*

Let yourself fall in love with your creativity like that and see what happens.

Stop treating your creativity like it's a tired, old, unhappy marriage (a grind, a drag) and start regarding it with the fresh eyes of a passionate lover. Even if you have only fifteen minutes a day in a stairwell alone with your creativity, take it. Go hide in that stairwell and make out with your art! (You can get a lot of making out done in fifteen minutes, as any furtive teenager can tell you.) Sneak off and have an affair with your most creative self. Lie to everyone about where you're actually going on your lunch break. Pretend you're traveling on a business trip when secretly you're retreating in order to paint, or to write poetry, or to draw up the plans for your future organic mushroom farm. Conceal it from your family and friends, whatever it is you're up to. Slip away from everyone else at the party and go off to dance alone with your ideas in the dark. Wake yourself up in the middle of the night in order to be alone with your inspiration, while nobody is watching. You don't need that sleep right now; you can give it up.

What else are you willing to give up in order to be alone with your beloved?

Don't think of it all as burdensome; think of it all as *sexy*.

Tristram Shandy Chimes In

Also, try to present yourself to your creativity as if *you* are sexy—as if you are somebody worth spending time with. I've always taken delight on this point from the novel *Tristram Shandy*, written by Laurence Sterne, eighteenth-century British essayist, novelist, and general man about town. In the novel, Tristram presents what I see as a marvelous cure for writer's block—to dress up in his finest regalia and act all princely, thus attracting ideas and inspiration to his side on account of his fabulous ensemble.

Specifically, here's what Tristram claims he would do when he was feeling "stupid" and blocked, and when his thoughts would "rise heavy and pass gummous through [his] pen." Instead of sitting there in a funk, staring hopelessly at the empty page, he would leap from the chair, get a fresh razor, and give himself a nice clean shave. ("How Homer could write with so long a beard I don't know.") After that, he would engage in this elaborate transformation: "I change my shirt—put on a better coat—send for my last wig—put my topaz ring upon my finger; and in a word, dress myself from one end to the other of me, after my best fashion."

Thus decked out to the nines, Tristram would strut around the room, presenting himself to the universe of creativity as appealingly as possible—looking every inch like a dashing suitor and a confident fellow. A charming trick, but best of all, it actually worked. As he explained: "A man cannot dress, but his ideas get cloth'd at the same time; and if he dresses like a gentleman, every one of them stands presented to his imagination."

I suggest that you try this trick at home.

I've done this myself sometimes, when I'm feeling particularly sluggish and useless, and when I feel like my creativity is hiding from me. I'll go look at myself in the mirror and say firmly, "Why *wouldn't* creativity hide from you, Gilbert? Look at yourself!"

Then I clean myself up. I take that goddamn scrunchie out of my greasy hair. I get out of those stale pajamas and take a shower. I shave—not my beard, but at least my legs. I put on some decent clothes. I brush my teeth, I wash my face. I put on lipstick—and I *never* wear lipstick. I clear my desk of its clutter, throw open a window, and maybe even light a scented candle. I might even put on perfume, for God's sake. I don't even put on perfume to go out to dinner, but I will put on perfume in an attempt to seduce creativity back to my side. (Coco Chanel: "A woman who doesn't wear perfume has no future.")

I always try to remind myself that I am having an affair with my creativity, and I make an effort to present myself to inspiration like somebody you might actually want to have an affair *with*—not like someone who's been wearing her husband's underwear around the house all week because she has totally given up. I put myself together from head to toe ("from one end to the other of me," in Tristram Shandy's words) and then I get back to my task. It works every time. Honest to God, if I had a freshly powdered eighteenth-century wig like Tristram's, I would wear it sometimes.

"Fake it till you make it" is the trick.

"Dress for the novel you *want* to write" is another way of saying it.

Seduce the Big Magic and it will always come back to you—the same way a raven is captivated by a shiny, spinning thing.

Fear in High Heels

I was once in love with a gifted young man—somebody who I thought was a far more talented writer than me—who decided in his twenties that he would not bother trying to be a writer after all, because the work never came out on the page quite as exquisitely as it lived in his head. He found it all too frustrating. He didn't want to sully the dazzling ideal that existed in his mind by putting a clumsy rendition of it down on paper.

While I beavered away at my awkward, disappointing short stories, this brilliant young man refused to write a word. He even tried to make me feel ashamed that I was attempting to write: Did the dreadful results not pain and offend me? He possessed a more pristine sense of artistic discernment, was the implication. Exposure to imperfections—even his own—injured his soul. He felt there was nobility in his choice never to write a book, if it could not be a great book.

He said, "I would rather be a beautiful failure than a deficient success."

Hell, I wouldn't.

The image of the tragic artist who lays down his tools

rather than fall short of his impeccable ideals holds no romance for me. I don't see this path as heroic. I think it's far more honorable to stay in the game—even if you're objectively failing at the game—than to excuse yourself from participation because of your delicate sensibilities. But in order to stay in the game, you must let go of your fantasy of perfection.

So let's talk for a moment about perfection.

The great American novelist Robert Stone once joked that he possessed the two worst qualities imaginable in a writer: He was lazy, and he was a perfectionist. Indeed, those are the essential ingredients for torpor and misery, right there. If you want to live a contented creative life, you do not want to cultivate either one of those traits, trust me. What you want is to cultivate quite the opposite: You must learn how to become a deeply disciplined half-ass.

It starts by forgetting about perfect. We don't have time for perfect. In any event, perfection is unachievable: It's a myth and a trap and a hamster wheel that will run you to death. The writer Rebecca Solnit puts it well: "So many of us believe in perfection, which ruins everything else, because the perfect is not only the enemy of the good; it's also the enemy of the realistic, the possible, and the fun."

Perfectionism stops people from completing their work, yes—but even worse, it often stops people from *beginning* their work. Perfectionists often decide in advance that the end product is never going to be satisfactory, so they don't even bother trying to be creative in the first place.

The most evil trick about perfectionism, though, is that it disguises itself as a virtue. In job interviews, for instance, people will sometimes advertise their perfectionism as if it's their greatest selling point—taking pride in the very thing that is holding them back from enjoying their fullest possible engagement with creative living. They wear their perfectionism like a badge of honor, as if it signals high tastes and exquisite standards.

But I see it differently. I think perfectionism is just a high-end, haute couture version of fear. I think perfectionism is just fear in fancy shoes and a mink coat, pretending to be elegant when actually it's just terrified. Because underneath that shiny veneer, perfectionism is nothing more than a deep existential angst that says, again and again, "I am not good enough and I will never be good enough."

Perfectionism is a particularly evil lure for women, who, I believe, hold themselves to an even higher standard of performance than do men. There are many reasons why women's voices and visions are not more widely represented today in creative fields. Some of that exclusion is due to regular old misogyny, but it's also true that—all too often—women are the ones holding themselves back from participating in the first place. Holding back their ideas, holding back their contributions, holding back their leadership and their talents. Too many women still seem to believe that they are not allowed to put themselves forward at all, until both they and their work are perfect and beyond criticism.

Meanwhile, putting forth work that is far from perfect *rarely stops men* from participating in the global cultural conversation. Just sayin'. And I don't say this as a criticism of men, by the way. I *like* that feature in men—their absurd overconfidence, the way they will casually decide, "Well, I'm 41 percent qualified for this task, so give me the job!" Yes, sometimes the results are ridiculous and disastrous, but sometimes, strangely enough, it works—a man who seems not ready for the task, not good enough for the task, somehow grows immediately into his potential through the wild leap of faith itself.

I only wish more women would risk these same kinds of wild leaps.

But I've watched too many women do the opposite. I've watched far too many brilliant and gifted female creators say, "I am 99.8 percent qualified for this task, but until I master that last smidgen of ability, I will hold myself back, just to be on the safe side."

Now, I cannot *imagine* where women ever got the idea

that they must be perfect in order to be loved or successful. (Ha ha ha! Just kidding! I can totally imagine: We got it from *every single message society has ever sent us!* Thanks, all of human history!) But we women must break this habit in ourselves—and we are the only ones who can break it. We must understand that the drive for perfectionism is a corrosive waste of time, because nothing is ever beyond criticism. No matter how many hours you spend attempting to render something flawless, somebody will always be able to find fault with it. (There are people out there who still consider Beethoven's symphonies a little bit too, you know, *loud*.) At some point, you really just have to finish your work and release it as is—if only so that you can go on to make other things with a glad and determined heart.

Which is the entire point.

Or should be.

Marcus Aurelius Chimes In

I've long been inspired by the private diaries of the second-century Roman emperor Marcus Aurelius. The wise philosopher-king never intended that his meditations be published, but I'm grateful that they were. I find it encouraging to watch this brilliant man, two thousand years ago, trying to keep up his motivation to be creative and brave and searching. His frustrations and his self-cajoling sound amazingly contemporary (or maybe just eternal and universal). You can hear him working through all the same questions that we all must work through in our lives: *Why am I here? What have I been called to do? How am I getting in my own way? How can I best live out my destiny?*

I especially love watching Marcus Aurelius fighting his perfectionism in order to get back to work on his writing, regardless of the results. "Do what nature demands," he writes to himself. "Get a move on—if you have it in you—and don't worry whether anyone will give you credit for it. And don't go expecting Plato's *Republic*; be satisfied with even the smallest progress, and treat the outcome of it all as unimportant."

Please tell me I'm not the only one who finds it endearing and encouraging that a legendary Roman philosopher had to reassure himself that *it's okay not to be Plato.*

Really, Marcus, it's okay!

Just keep working.

Through the mere act of creating something—anything—you might inadvertently produce work that is magnificent, eternal, or important (as Marcus Aurelius did, after all, with his *Meditations*). You might not, on the other hand. But if your calling is to make things, then you still have to make things in order to live out your highest creative potential—and also in order to remain sane. Possessing a creative mind, after all, is something like having a border collie for a pet: It needs to work, or else it will cause you an outrageous amount of trouble. Give your mind a job to do, or else it will find a job to do, and you might not like the job it invents (eating the couch, digging a hole through the living room floor, biting the mailman, etc.). It has taken me years to learn this, but it does seem to be the case that if I am not actively creating something, then I am probably actively destroying something (myself, a relationship, or my own peace of mind).

I firmly believe that we all need to find something to do in our lives that stops us from eating the couch. Whether we make a profession out of it or not, we all need an activity that is beyond the mundane and that takes us out of our established and limiting roles in society (mother, employee, neighbor, brother, boss, etc.). We all need something that helps us to forget ourselves for a while—to momentarily forget our age, our gender, our socioeconomic background, our duties, our failures, and all that we have lost and screwed up. We need something that takes us so far out of ourselves that we forget to eat, forget to pee, forget to mow the lawn, forget to resent our enemies, forget to brood over our insecurities. Prayer can do that for us, community service can do it, sex can do it, exercise can do it, and substance abuse can most certainly do it (albeit with god-awful consequences)—but creative living can do it, too. Perhaps creativity's greatest mercy is this: By completely absorbing our attention for a short and magical spell, it can relieve us temporarily from the dreadful burden of being who we are. Best of all, at the end of your creative adventure, you have a souvenir—something that you *made*, something to remind you forever of your brief but transformative encounter with inspiration.

That's what my books are to me: souvenirs of journeys

that I took, in which I managed (blessedly) to escape myself for a little while.

An abiding stereotype of creativity is that it turns people crazy. I disagree: *Not* expressing creativity turns people crazy. ("If you bring forth what is within you, what you bring forth will save you. If you don't bring forth what is within you, what you don't bring forth will destroy you." —Gospel of Thomas.) Bring forth what is within you, then, whether it succeeds or fails. Do it whether the final product (your souvenir) is crap or gold. Do it whether the critics love you or hate you—or whether the critics have never heard of you and perhaps never will hear of you. Do it whether people get it or don't get it.

It doesn't have to be perfect, and you don't have to be Plato.

It's all just an instinct and an experiment and a mystery, so begin.

Begin anywhere. Preferably right now.

And if greatness should ever accidentally stumble upon you, let it catch you hard at work.

Hard at work, and sane.

Nobody's Thinking About You

Long ago, when I was in my insecure twenties, I met a clever, independent, creative, and powerful woman in her mid-seventies, who offered me a superb piece of life wisdom.

She said: "We all spend our twenties and thirties trying so hard to be perfect, because we're so worried about what people will think of us. Then we get into our forties and fifties, and we finally start to be free, because we decide that we don't give a damn what anyone thinks of us. But you won't be completely free until you reach your sixties and seventies, when you finally realize this liberating truth—*nobody was ever thinking about you, anyhow.*"

They aren't. They weren't. They never were.

People are mostly just thinking about themselves. People don't have time to worry about what you're doing, or how well you're doing it, because they're all caught up in their own dramas. People's attention may be drawn to you for a moment (if you succeed or fail spectacularly and publicly, for instance), but that attention will soon enough revert right back to where it's always been—*on themselves.* While it may seem lonely and horrible at first to imagine that you aren't anyone else's first order of business, there is also a great release to be found in this idea. You are free, because everyone is too busy fussing over themselves to worry all that much about you.

Go be whomever you want to be, then.

Do whatever you want to do.

Pursue whatever fascinates you and brings you to life.

Create whatever you want to create—and let it be stupendously imperfect, because it's exceedingly likely that nobody will even notice.

And that's *awesome.*

Done Is Better Than Good

The only reason I was able to persist in completing my first novel was that I allowed it to be stupendously imperfect. I pushed myself to continue writing it, even though I strongly disapproved of what I was producing. That book was so far from perfect, it made me nuts. I remember pacing around in my room during the years that I worked on the novel, trying to gin up my courage to return to that lackluster manuscript every single day, despite its awfulness, reminding myself of this vow: "I never promised the universe that I would be a *great* writer, goddamn it! I just promised the universe that I would be a *writer*!"

At seventy-five pages in, I nearly stopped. It felt too terrible to continue, too deeply embarrassing. But I pushed through my own shame only because I decided that I *refused* to go to my grave with seventy-five pages of an unfinished manuscript sitting in my desk drawer. I did not want to be that person. The world is filled with too many unfinished manuscripts as it is, and I didn't want to add another one to that bottomless pile. So no matter how much I thought my work stank, I had to persist.

I also kept remembering what my mother always used to say: "Done is better than good."

I heard that simple adage of my mother's again and again the entire time I was growing up. This was not because Carole Gilbert was a slacker. On the contrary, she was incredibly industrious and efficient—but more than anything else, she was pragmatic. There are only so many hours in a day, after all. There are only so many days in a year, only so many years in a life. You do what you can do, as competently as possible within a reasonable time frame, and then you let it go. When it came to everything from washing the dishes to wrapping Christmas presents, my mother's thinking was much in line with General George Patton's: "A good plan violently executed now is better than a perfect plan executed next week."

Or, to paraphrase: A good-enough novel violently written now is better than a perfect novel meticulously written never.

I also think my mother understood this radical notion—that mere completion is a rather honorable achievement in its own right. What's more, it's a rare one. Because the truth of the matter is, most people don't finish things! Look around you, the evidence is everywhere: *People don't finish.* They begin ambitious projects with the best of intentions, but then they get stuck in a mire of insecurity and doubt and hairsplitting . . . and they stop.

So if you can just complete something—merely complete it!—you're already miles ahead of the pack, right there.

You may want your work to be perfect, in other words; I just want mine to be finished.

In Praise of Crooked Houses

I could sit down with you right now and go through each of my books, page by page, and tell you everything that's wrong with them. This would make for an incredibly boring afternoon for both of us, but I could do it. I could show you everything that I elected not to fix, change, improve, or fuss over. I could show you every shortcut I took when I couldn't figure out how to more elegantly solve a complicated narrative puzzle. I could show you characters I killed off because I didn't know what else to do with them. I could show you gaps in logic and holes in research. I could show you all kinds of sticky tape and shoelaces holding those projects together.

To save time, though, let me offer just one representative example. In my most recent novel, *The Signature of All Things*, there is an unfortunately underdeveloped character. She is rather egregiously improbable (I believe, anyhow), and her presence is little more than a convenience to the plot. I knew in my heart—even as I was writing her—that I did not get this character quite right, but I couldn't figure out how to bring her to life better, as I should have. I was hoping to get away with it. Sometimes you do get away with things. I was hoping nobody would notice. But then I gave the book to some of my early readers while the book was still in manuscript, and they all pointed out the problem with this character.

I considered trying to fix it. But what it would have taken for me to go back and remedy that one character was too much effort for not enough reward. For one thing, fixing this character would've required adding an additional fifty or seventy pages to a manuscript that was already over seven hundred pages long—and at some point, you really have to show mercy to your readers and cut the thing off. I also felt it was too risky. To solve the problem of this character, I would've had to dismantle the entire novel back down to the early chapters and start over—and in rebuilding the story so radically, I feared, I might end up destroying a book that was already done, and was already *good enough*. It would be like a carpenter tearing down a finished house and completely starting over because he'd noticed—at the very end of the construction project—that the foundation was off by a few inches. Sure, by the end of the second construction, the foundation might be straighter, but the charm of the original structure might have been destroyed, while months of time had been wasted.

I decided not to do it.

In short, I'd worked on that novel tirelessly for four years, had given it a tremendous amount of effort, love, and faith, and basically I liked it the way it was. Yes, there was some crookedness, but the walls were essentially strong, the roof held, and the windows functioned, and anyhow, I don't entirely mind living in a crooked house. (I grew up in a crooked house; they aren't such bad places.) I felt that my novel was an interesting finished product—maybe even more interesting for its slightly wonky angles—so I let it go.

And do you know what happened when I released my admittedly imperfect book into the world?

Not much.

The earth stayed on its axis. Rivers did not run backward. Birds didn't drop dead out of the air. I got some good reviews, some bad reviews, some indifferent reviews. Some people loved *The Signature of All Things*, some people didn't. A plumber who came over one day to repair my kitchen sink noticed the book sitting on the table and said, "I can tell you right now, lady, that book ain't gonna sell—not with *that* title." Some people wished the novel had been shorter; others wished it were longer. Some readers wished the story had more dogs in it and less masturbation. A few critics made note of that one underdeveloped character, but nobody seemed overly bothered by her.

In conclusion: A whole bunch of people had some opinions about my novel for a short while, and then everyone moved on, because people are busy and they have their own lives to think about. But I'd had a thrilling intellectual and emotional experience writing *The Signature of All Things*—and the merits of that creative adventure were mine to keep forever. Those four years of my life had been wonderfully well spent. When I finished that novel, it was not a perfect thing, but I still felt it was the best work I'd ever done, and I believed I was a far better writer than I'd been before I began it. I would not trade a minute of that encounter for anything.

But now that work was finished, and it was time for me to shift my attention to something new—something that would also, someday, be released as *good enough.* This is how I've always done it, and this is how I will keep doing it, so long as I am able.

Because that is the anthem of my people.

That is the Song of the Disciplined Half-Ass.

Success

All those years when I was diligently laboring away at both my day jobs and my writing practice, I knew there was never any promise that any of this would work out.

I always knew that I might not get what I wished for—that I might never become a published writer. Not everybody makes it to a place of comfortable success in the arts. Most people don't. And while I've always believed in magical thinking, I wasn't a child, either; I knew that wishing would not make it so. Talent might not make it so, either. Dedication might not make it so. Even amazing professional contacts—which I didn't have, in any case—might not make it so.

Creative living is stranger than other, more worldly pursuits. The usual rules do not apply. In normal life, if you're good at something and you work hard at it, you will likely succeed. In creative endeavors, maybe not. Or maybe you will succeed for a spell, and then never succeed again. You might be offered rewards on a silver platter, even as a rug is being simultaneously pulled out from under you. You might be adored for a while, then go out of fashion.

Other, dumber people might take your place as critical darlings.

The patron goddess of creative success can sometimes seem like a rich, capricious old lady who lives in a giant mansion on a distant hill and who makes really weird decisions about who gets her fortune. She sometimes rewards charlatans and ignores the gifted. She cuts people out of her will who loyally served her for their entire lives, and then gives a Mercedes to that cute boy who cut her lawn once. She changes her mind about things. We try to divine her motives, but they remain occult. She is never obliged to explain herself to us. In short, the goddess of creative success may show up for you, or she may not. Probably best, then, if you don't count on her, or attach your definition of personal happiness to her whims.

Maybe better to reconsider your definition of success, period.

For my own part, I decided early on to focus on my devotion to the work above all. That would be how I measured my worth. I knew that conventional success would depend upon three factors—talent, luck, and discipline—and I knew that two of those three things would never be under my control. Genetic randomness had already determined how much talent I'd been allotted, and destiny's randomness would account for my share of luck. The only piece I had any control over was my discipline. Recognizing that, it seemed like the best plan would be to work my ass off. That was the only card I had to play, so I played it hard.

Mind you, hard work guarantees *nothing* in realms of creativity. (Nothing guarantees anything in realms of creativity.) But I cannot help but think that devotional discipline is the best approach. Do what you love to do, and do it with both seriousness and lightness. At least then you will know that you have tried and that—whatever the outcome—you have traveled a noble path.

I have a friend, an aspiring musician, whose sister said to her one day, quite reasonably, "What happens if you never get anything out of this? What happens if you pursue your passion forever, but success never comes? How will you feel then, having wasted your entire life for nothing?"

My friend, with equal reason, replied, "If you can't see what I'm *already* getting out of this, then I'll never be able to explain it to you."

When it's for love, you will always do it anyhow.

Career vs. Vocation

It is for these reasons (the difficulty, the unpredictability) that I have always discouraged people from approaching creativity as a career move, and I always will—because, with rare exceptions, creative fields make for crap careers. (They make for crap careers, that is, if you define a "career" as something that provides for you financially in a fair and foreseeable manner, which is a pretty reasonable definition of a career.)

Even if things work out for you in the arts, parts of your career will likely always remain crap. You might not like your publisher, or your gallerist, or your drummer, or your cinematographer. You might hate your tour schedule, or your more aggressive fans, or your critics. You might resent answering the same questions over and over again in interviews. You might be constantly annoyed at yourself for always falling short of your own aspirations. Trust me, if you want to complain, you'll always find plenty to complain about, even when fortune appears to be shining her favor upon you.

But creative living can be an amazing *vocation*, if you have the love and courage and persistence to see it that way. I suggest that this may be the only sanity-preserving way to approach creativity. Because nobody ever told us it would be easy, and uncertainty is what we sign up for when we say that we want to live creative lives.

Everyone is panicking these days, for instance, about how much the Internet and digital technology are changing the creative world. Everyone is fretting over whether there will still be jobs and money available for artists going forward into this volatile new age. But allow me to point out that—long before the Internet and digital technology ever existed—the arts were still a crap career. It's not like back in 1989 anybody was saying to me, "You know where the money is, kid? *Writing!*" They weren't saying that to anyone back in 1889, either, or in 1789, and they won't be saying it in 2089. But people will still try to be writers, because they love the vocation. People will keep being painters, sculptors, musicians, actors, poets, directors, quilters, knitters, potters, glassblowers, metalworkers, ceramicists, calligraphers, collagists, nail artists, clog dancers, and Celtic harpists, as well. Against all sound advice, people will stubbornly keep trying to make pleasing things for no particularly good reason, as we always have done.

Is it sometimes a difficult path? Sure.

Does it make for an interesting life? The most.

Will the inevitable difficulties and obstacles associated

with creativity make you suffer? That part—cross my heart—is entirely up to you.

Elk Talk

Let me tell you a story about persistence and patience.

Back in my early twenties, I wrote a short story called "Elk Talk." The tale had grown out of an experience I'd had back when I was working as a cook on a ranch in Wyoming. One evening, I had stayed up late telling jokes and drinking beer with a few of the cowboys. These guys were all hunters, and we got to talking about elk calls—the various techniques for imitating a bull elk's mating call in order to draw the animals near. One of the cowboys, Hank, admitted that he had recently purchased a tape recording of some elk calls made by the greatest master of elk-calling in elk-hunting history, a guy named (and I will never forget this) Larry D. Jones.

For some reason—it might have been the beer—I thought this was the funniest thing I'd ever heard. I loved that there was somebody in the world named Larry D. Jones who made a living by recording himself imitating mating calls of elks, and I loved that people like my friend

Hank bought these tapes in order to practice their own mating calls. I persuaded Hank to go find the Larry D. Jones instructional mating-call tape, and I made him play it for me again and again while I laughed myself dizzy. It wasn't just the sound of the elk call that I found hilarious (it's an eardrum-shredding Styrofoam-against-Styrofoam screech); I also loved the earnest twang of Larry D. Jones droning on and on about how to do it correctly. I found the whole thing to be comedy gold.

Then somehow (again, the beer may have played a role) I got this idea that Hank and I should go try it out—that we should stumble into the woods in the middle of the night with a boom box and the Larry D. Jones tape, just to see what would happen. So we did. We were drunk and giddy and loud as we thrashed through the Wyoming mountains. Hank carried the boom box on his shoulder and turned up the volume as high as he could, while I kept falling over laughing at the loud, artificial sound of a bull elk in rut—interspersed with Larry D. Jones's droning voice—blasting through our surroundings.

We could not have been less in tune with nature at that moment, but nature found us anyway. All at once there was a thunder of hooves (I'd never heard an actual thunder of hooves before; it's terrifying) and then a crashing of branches, and then the biggest elk you ever saw exploded into our clearing and stood there in the moonlight, just a few short yards from us, snorting and pawing at the ground and tossing his antlered head in fury: *What rival male has dared to bugle a mating call on my turf?*

Suddenly, Larry D. Jones didn't seem so funny anymore.

Never have two people sobered up as fast as Hank and I sobered up right then. We'd been kidding, but this seven-hundred-pound beast was decidedly not kidding. He was ready for war. It was as if we'd been conducting a harmless little séance, but had inadvertently summoned forth an actual dangerous spirit. We'd been messing around with forces that should not be messed with, and we were not worthy.

My impulse was to bow down before the elk, trembling, and to beg for mercy. Hank's impulse was smarter—to throw the boom box as far away from us as he could, as if it were about to detonate (anything to distance ourselves from the bogus voice that we had dragged into this all-too-real forest). We cowered behind a boulder. We gawped at the elk in wonder while it blew clouds of frosty breath, furiously looking for its rival, tearing up the earth beneath its hooves. When you see the face of God, it is meant to frighten you, and this magnificent creature had frightened us in exactly that manner.

When the elk finally departed, we inched our way back

to the ranch, feeling humbled and shaken and very mortal. It was *awesome*—in the classical definition of the word.

So I wrote about it. I didn't tell this exact story, but I wanted to catch hold of that sensation ("callow humans humbled by divine natural visitation") and use it as the basis for writing something serious and intense about man and nature. I wanted to take that electrifying personal experience and work it into a piece of short fiction using imagined characters. It took me many months to get that story right—or at least to get it as close to right as I possibly could, for my age and abilities. When I finished writing the story, I called it "Elk Talk." Then I started sending it out to magazines, hoping somebody would publish it.

One of the publications that I sent "Elk Talk" to was the late, great fiction journal *Story*. Many of my literary heroes—Cheever, Caldwell, Salinger, Heller—had been published there over the decades, and I wanted to be in those pages, too. A few weeks later, my inevitable rejection letter arrived in the post. But this was a really special rejection letter.

You have to understand that rejection letters come in varying degrees, ranging across the full spectrum of the word *no*. There is not only the boilerplate form rejection letter; there is also the boilerplate rejection letter with a tiny personal note scrawled on the bottom, in an actual human's handwriting, which might say something like, *Interesting, but not for us!* It can be exhilarating to receive even such a sparse crumb of recognition, and many times in my youth I'd been known to run around crowing to my friends, "I just got the most *amazing* rejection note!"

But this particular rejection letter was from *Story*'s well-respected editor in chief, Lois Rosenthal herself. Her response was thoughtful and encouraging. Ms. Rosenthal liked the story, she wrote. She tended to like stories about animals better than stories about people. Ultimately, however, she felt that the ending fell short. Therefore, she would not be publishing it. But she wished me good luck.

To an unpublished writer, getting rejected as nicely as that—from the editor in chief herself!—is almost like winning the Pulitzer. I was elated. It was by far the most fantastic rejection I'd ever received. And then I did what I used to do all the time back then: I took that rejected short story out of its self-addressed stamped envelope and sent it off to another magazine to collect yet another rejection letter—maybe an even better one. Because that is how you play the game. Onward ever, backward never.

A few years passed. I kept working at my day jobs and writing on the side. I finally did get published—with a different short story, in a different magazine. Because of that lucky break, I was now able to get a professional literary agent. Now it was my agent, Sarah, who sent my work out to publishers on my behalf. (No more photocopying for me; my agent had her own photocopier!) A few months into our relationship, Sarah called me with lovely news: My old short story "Elk Talk" was going to be published.

"Wonderful," I said. "Who bought it?"

"*Story* magazine," she reported. "Lois Rosenthal loved it."

Huh.

Interesting.

A few days later, I had a phone conversation with Lois herself, who could not have been kinder. She told me that she thought "Elk Talk" was perfect, and that she couldn't wait to publish it.

"You even liked the ending?" I asked.

"Of course," she said. "I adore the ending."

As we spoke, I was holding in my hands the very rejection letter she had written me just a few years earlier about this same story. Clearly, she had no recollection of ever having read "Elk Talk" before. I didn't bring it up. I was delighted that she was embracing my work, and I didn't want to seem disrespectful, snarky, or ungrateful. But I certainly was curious, so I asked, "What is it that you like about my story, if you don't mind telling me?"

She said, "It's so evocative. It feels mythical. It reminds

me of something, but I can't quite put my finger on what . . ."

I knew better than to say, "It reminds you of *itself.*"

The Beautiful Beast

So how do we interpret this tale?

The cynical interpretation would be "This is unequivocal evidence that the world is a place of deep unfairness."

Because look at the facts: Lois Rosenthal didn't want "Elk Talk" when it was submitted to her by an unknown author, but she did want it when it was submitted to her by a famous literary agent. Therefore: It's not what you know, it's who you know. Talent means nothing, and connections mean everything, and the world of creativity—like the greater world itself—is a mean and unfair place.

If you want to see it that way, go right ahead.

But I didn't see it that way. On the contrary, I saw it as another example of Big Magic—and, again, a witty one. I saw it as proof that you must never surrender, that no doesn't always mean *no*, and that miraculous turns of fate can happen to those who persist in showing up.

Also, just try to imagine how many short stories a day Lois Rosenthal was reading back in the early 1990s. (I've seen slush piles at magazines; picture a tower of manila envelopes stacked up to the sky.) We all like to think that our work is original and unforgettable, but surely it must all run together after a certain point—even the animal-themed stories. Moreover, I don't know what kind of mood Lois was in when she read "Elk Talk" the first time. She might have read it at the end of a long day, or after an argument with a colleague, or just before she had to drive to the airport to pick up a relative she wasn't looking forward to seeing. I don't know what sort of mood she was in when she read it for the second time, either. Maybe she'd just come back from a restorative vacation. Maybe she'd just received elating news: A loved one didn't have cancer, after all! Who knows? All I do know is that, when Lois Rosenthal read my short story for the second time, it echoed in her consciousness and sang out to her. But that echo was only in her mind because *I had planted it there*, several years earlier, by sending her my story in the first place. And also because I had stayed in the game, even after the initial rejection.

This event also taught me that these people—the ones who stand at the gates of our dreams—are not automatons. They are just *people*. They are just like us. They are whimsical and quirky. They're a little different every day, just as you and I are a little different every day. There is no neat template that can ever predict what will capture any one person's imagination, or when; you just have to reach them at the right moment. But since the right moment is unknowable, you must maximize your chances. Play the odds. Put yourself forward in stubborn good cheer, and then do it again and again and again . . .

The effort is worth it, because when at last you do connect, it is an otherworldly delight of the highest order. Because this is how it feels to lead the faithful creative life: You try and try and try, and nothing works. But you keep trying, and you keep seeking, and then sometimes, in the least expected place and time, it finally happens. You make the connection. Out of nowhere, it all comes together. Making art does sometimes feel like you're holding a séance, or like you're calling out in the night for a wild animal on the prowl. What you're doing seems impossible and even silly, but then you hear the thunder of hooves, and some beautiful beast comes rushing into the glade, searching for you just as urgently as you have been searching for it.

So you must keep trying. You must keep calling out in those dark woods for your own Big Magic. You must search tirelessly and faithfully, hoping against hope to someday experience that divine collision of creative communion—either for the first time, or one more time.

Because when it all comes together, it's amazing. When it all comes together, the only thing you can do is bow down in gratitude, as if you have been granted an audience with the divine.

Because you have.

Lastly, This

Many years ago, my uncle Nick went to see the eminent American writer Richard Ford give a talk at a bookstore in Washington, DC. During the Q&A after the reading, a middle-aged man in the audience stood up and said something like this:

"Mr. Ford, you and I have much in common. Just like you, I have been writing short stories and novels my whole life. You and I are about the same age, from the same background, and we write about the same themes. The only difference is that you have become a celebrated man of letters, and I—despite decades of effort—have never been published. This is heartbreaking to me. My spirit has been crushed by all the rejection and disappointment. I wonder if you have any advice for me. But please, sir, whatever you do, don't just tell me to persevere, because that's the only thing people ever tell me to do, and hearing that only makes me feel worse."

Now, I wasn't there. And I don't know Richard Ford personally. But according to my uncle, who is a good reporter, Ford replied, "Sir, I am sorry for your disappointment. Please believe me, I would never insult you by simply telling you to persevere. I can't even imagine how discouraging that would be to hear, after all these years of rejection. In fact, I will tell you something else—something that may surprise you. I'm going to tell you to quit."

The audience froze: What kind of encouragement was this?

Ford went on: "I say this to you only because writing is clearly bringing you no pleasure. It is only bringing you pain. Our time on earth is short and should be enjoyed. You should leave this dream behind and go find something else to do with your life. Travel, take up new hobbies, spend time with your family and friends, relax. But don't write anymore, because it's obviously killing you."

There was a long silence.

Then Ford smiled and added, almost as an afterthought:

"However, I will say this. If you happen to discover, after a few years away from writing, that you have found nothing that takes its place in your life—nothing that fascinates you, or moves you, or inspires you to the same degree that writing once did . . . well, then, sir, I'm afraid you will have no choice but to persevere."

Trust

Does It Love You?

My friend Dr. Robin Wall Kimmerer is a botanist and an author who teaches environmental biology at the SUNY College of Environmental Science and Forestry in Syracuse, New York. Her students are all fervent young environmentalists, earnest as can be, desperate to save the world.

Before they can get down to the business of world-saving, though, Robin often asks her students these two questions.

The first question is: "Do you love nature?"

Every hand in the room goes up.

The second question is: "Do you believe that nature loves you in return?"

Every hand in the room goes down.

At which point Robin says, "Then we have a problem already."

The problem is this: These earnest young world-savers honestly believe that the living earth is indifferent to them. They believe that humans are nothing but passive consumers, and that our presence here on earth is a destructive force. (We take, take, take and offer nothing of benefit to nature in return.) They believe that humans are here on this planet by random accident, and that therefore the earth doesn't give a damn about us.

Ancient people did not see it this way, needless to say. Our ancestors always operated with a sense of being in a reciprocal emotional relationship with their physical surroundings. Whether they felt that they were being rewarded by Mother Nature or punished by her, at least they were engaged in a constant *conversation* with her.

Robin believes that modern people have lost that sense of conversation—lost that awareness of the earth communicating with *us* just as much as we are communicating with *it*. Instead, modern people have been schooled to believe that nature is deaf and blind to them—perhaps because we believe that nature has no inherent sentience. Which is a somewhat pathological construct, because it denies any possibility of relationship. (Even the notion of a punitive Mother Earth is better than the notion of an indifferent one—because at least anger represents some sort of energetic exchange.)

Without that sense of relationship, Robin warns her students, they are missing out on something incredibly important: They are missing out on their potential to become *cocreators* of life. As Robin puts it, "The exchange of love between earth and people calls forth the creative gifts of both. The earth is not indifferent to us, but rather calling for our gifts in return for hers—the reciprocal nature of life and creativity."

Or, to put it more simply: Nature provides the seed; man provides the garden; each is grateful for the other's help.

So Robin always begins right there. Before she can teach these students how to heal the world, she has to teach them how to heal *their notion of themselves in the world*. She has to convince them of their right to even be here at all. (Again: the arrogance of belonging.) She has to introduce them to the concept that they might actually be loved in return by the very entity that they themselves revere—by nature itself, by the very entity that created them.

Because otherwise it's never going to work.

Because otherwise nobody—not the earth, not the students, not any us—will ever benefit.

Worst Girlfriend Ever

Inspired by this notion, I now often ask aspiring young writers the same line of questions.

"Do you love writing?" I ask.

Of course they do. *Duh.*

Then I ask: "Do you believe that writing loves you in return?"

They look at me like I should be institutionalized.

"Of course not," they say. Most of them report that writing is totally indifferent to them. And if they do happen to feel a reciprocal relationship with their creativity, it is usually a deeply sick relationship. In many cases, these young writers claim that writing flat-out hates them. Writing messes with their heads. Writing torments them and hides from them. Writing punishes them. Writing destroys them. Writing kicks their asses, ten ways to Sunday.

As one young writer I know put it, "For me, writing is like that bitchy, beautiful girl in high school who you always worshipped, but who only toyed with you for her own purposes. You know in your heart that she's bad news, and you should probably just walk away from her forever, but she always lures you back in. Just when you think she's finally going to be your girlfriend, she shows up at school holding hands with the captain of the football team, pretending she's never met you. All you can do is weep in a locked bathroom stall. Writing is *evil.*"

"That being the case," I asked him, "what do you want to do with your life?"

"I want to be a writer," he said.

Addicted to Suffering

Are you beginning to see how screwed-up this is?

It is not only aspiring writers who feel this way. Older, established authors say exactly the same dark things about their own work. (Where do you think the young writers learned it from?) Norman Mailer claimed that every one of his books had killed him a little more. Philip Roth has never stopped talking about the medieval torments writing inflicted upon him for the duration of his long-suffering career. Oscar Wilde called the artistic existence "one long, lovely suicide." (I adore Wilde, but I have trouble seeing suicide as lovely. I have trouble seeing any of this anguish as lovely.)

And it's not just writers who feel this way. Visual artists

do it, too. Here's the painter Francis Bacon: "The feelings of desperation and unhappiness are more useful to an artist than the feeling of contentment, because desperation and unhappiness stretch your whole sensibility." Actors do it, dancers do it, and musicians most certainly do it. Rufus Wainwright once admitted that he was terrified to settle down into a happy relationship, because without the emotional drama that came from all those dysfunctional love affairs, he was afraid of losing access to "that dark lake of pain" he felt was so critical to his music.

And let's not even get started on the poets.

Suffice it to say that the modern language of creativity—from its youngest aspirants up to its acknowledged masters—is steeped in pain, desolation, and dysfunction. Numberless artists toil away in total emotional and physical solitude—disassociated not only from other humans, but also from the source of creativity itself.

Worse, their relationship with their work is often emotionally violent. You want to make something? You are told to open up a vein and bleed. Time to edit your work? You are instructed to kill your darlings. Ask a writer how his book is going, and he might say, "I finally broke its spine this week."

And that's if he had a *good* week.

A Cautionary Tale

One of the most interesting up-and-coming novelists I know these days is a clever young woman named Katie Arnold-Ratliff. Katie writes like a dream. But she told me that she'd gotten blocked from her work for several years because of something a writing professor had said to her: "Unless you are emotionally uncomfortable while you are writing, you will never produce anything of value."

Now, there's a level at which I understand what Katie's writing professor might have been trying to say. Perhaps the intended message was "Don't be afraid of reaching for your creative edge," or "Never back away from the discomfort that can sometimes arise while you're working." These seem like perfectly legitimate notions to me. But to suggest that nobody ever made valuable art unless they were in active emotional distress is not only untrue, it's also kind of sick.

But Katie believed it.

Out of respect and deference to her professor, Katie took those words to heart and came to embrace the notion that if her creative process wasn't bringing her anguish, then she wasn't doing it right.

No blood, no glory, right?

The problem was, Katie had an idea for a novel that actually made her feel excited. The book she wanted to write seemed so cool, so twisted, and so strange that she thought it might genuinely be fun to do it. In fact, it seemed like so much fun, it made her feel guilty. Because if something was a pleasure to write, then it couldn't possibly have any artistic value, could it?

So she put off writing that cool and twisted novel of hers for years and years, because she didn't trust in the legitimacy of her own anticipated pleasure. Eventually, I am happy to report, she broke through that mental obstacle and finally wrote her book. And, no, it was not necessarily *easy* to write, but she did have a great time writing it. And yes, it is brilliant.

What a pity, though, to have lost all those years of inspired creativity—and only because she didn't believe her work was making her miserable enough!

Yeah.

Heaven forbid anyone should enjoy their chosen vocation.

The Teaching of Pain

Sadly, Katie's story is no anomaly.

Far too many creative people have been taught to distrust pleasure and to put their faith in struggle alone. Too many artists still believe that anguish is the only truly authentic emotional experience. They could have picked up this dark idea anywhere; it's a commonly held belief here in the Western world, what with our weighty emotional heritage of Christian sacrifice and German Romanticism—both of which give excessive credence to the merits of agony.

Trusting in nothing but suffering is a dangerous path, though. Suffering has a reputation for killing off artists, for one thing. But even when it doesn't kill them, an addiction to pain can sometimes throw artists into such severe mental disorder that they stop working at all. (My favorite refrigerator magnet: "I've suffered enough. When does my artwork improve?")

Perhaps you, too, were taught to trust in darkness.

Maybe you were even taught darkness by creative people whom you loved and admired. I certainly was. When I was in high school, a beloved English teacher once told me,

"You're a talented writer, Liz. But unfortunately you'll never make it, because you haven't suffered enough in your life."

What a twisted thing to say!

First of all, what does a middle-aged man know about a teenage girl's suffering? I had probably suffered more that day at *lunch* than he'd ever suffered in his entire lifetime. But beyond that—since when did creativity become a suffering contest?

I had admired that teacher. Imagine if I'd taken his words to heart and had dutifully set out on some shadowy Byronic quest for authenticating tribulation. Mercifully, I didn't. My instincts drove me in the opposite direction—toward light, toward play, toward a more trusting engagement with creativity—but I'm a lucky one. Others do go on that dark crusade, and sometimes they go there on purpose. "All my musical heroes were junkies, and I just wanted to be one, too," says my dear friend Rayya Elias, a gifted songwriter who battled heroin addiction for over a decade, during which time she lived in prison, on the streets, and in mental hospitals—and completely stopped making music.

Rayya isn't the only artist who ever mistook self-destruction for a serious-minded commitment to creativity. The jazz saxophonist Jackie McLean said that—back in Greenwich Village in the 1950s—he watched dozens of aspiring young musicians take up heroin in order to imitate their hero, Charlie Parker. More tellingly still, McLean says, he witnessed many young jazz aspirants *pretending* to be heroin addicts ("eyes half-closed, striking that slouched pose") even as Parker himself begged people not to emulate this most tragic aspect of himself. But maybe it's easier to do heroin—or even to romantically pretend to do heroin—than it is to commit yourself wholeheartedly to your craft.

Addiction does not make the artist. Raymond Carver, for one, intimately knew this to be true. He himself was an alcoholic, and he was never able to become the writer he needed to be—not even on the subject of alcoholism itself—until he gave up the booze. As he said, "Any artist who is an alcoholic is an artist *despite* their alcoholism, not because of it."

I agree. I believe that our creativity grows like sidewalk weeds out of the cracks between our pathologies—not from the pathologies themselves. But so many people think it's the other way around. For this reason, you will often meet artists who deliberately cling to their suffering, their addictions, their fears, their demons. They worry that if they ever let go of all that anguish, their very identities would vanish. Think of Rilke, who famously said, "If my devils are to leave me, I'm afraid my angels will take flight, as well."

Rilke was a glorious poet, and that line is elegantly rendered, but it's also severely emotionally warped. Unfortunately, I've heard that line quoted countless times by creative people who were offering up an excuse as to why they won't quit drinking, or why they won't go see a therapist, or why they won't consider treatment for their depression or anxiety, or why they won't address their sexual misconduct or their intimacy problems, or why they basically refuse to seek personal healing and growth in any manner whatsoever—*because they don't want to lose their suffering*, which they have somehow conflated and confused with their creativity.

People have a strange trust in their devils, indeed.

Our Better Angels

I want to make something perfectly clear here: I do not deny the reality of suffering—not yours, not mine, not humanity's in general. It is simply that I refuse to *fetishize* it. I certainly refuse to deliberately seek out suffering in the name of artistic authenticity. As Wendell Berry warned, "To attribute to the Muse a special fondness for pain is to come too close to desiring and cultivating pain."

To be sure, the Tormented Artist is sometimes an all-too-real person. Without a doubt, there are many creative souls out there who suffer from severe mental illness. (Then again, there are also hundreds of thousands of severely mentally ill souls out there who do not happen to possess extraordinary artistic talents, so to automatically conflate madness with genius feels like a logical fallacy to me.) But we must be wary of the lure of the Tormented Artist, because sometimes it's a *persona*—a role that people grow accustomed to playing. It can be a seductively picturesque role, too, with a certain dark and romantic glamour to it. And it comes with an extremely useful side benefit—namely, built-in permission for terrible behavior.

If you are the Tormented Artist, after all, then you have an excuse for treating your romantic partners badly, for treating yourself badly, for treating your children badly, for treating everyone badly. You are allowed to be demanding, arrogant, rude, cruel, antisocial, grandiose, explosive, moody, manipulative, irresponsible, and/or selfish. You can drink all day and fight all night. If you behaved this badly as a janitor or a pharmacist, people would rightfully call you out as a jackass. But as the Tormented Artist, you get a pass, because you're special. Because you're sensitive and creative. Because sometimes you make pretty things.

I don't buy it. I believe you can live a creative life and

still make an effort to be a basically decent person. I'm with the British psychoanalyst Adam Phillips on this point, when he observes: "If the art legitimates cruelty, I think the art is not worth having."

I've never been attracted to the icon of the Tormented Artist—not even during adolescence, when that figure can seem particularly sexy and alluring to romantic-minded girls like me. It never appealed to me then, though, and it still doesn't appeal to me now. What I've seen already of pain is plenty, thank you, and I do not raise my hand and ask for more of it. I've also been around enough mentally ill people to know better than to sentimentalize madness. What's more, I've passed through enough seasons of depression, anxiety, and shame in my own life to know that such experiences are not particularly generative for me. I have no great love or loyalty for my personal devils, because they have never served me well. During my own periods of misery and instability, I've noticed that my creative spirit becomes cramped and suffocated. I've found that it's nearly impossible for me to write when I am unhappy, and it is *definitely* impossible for me to write fiction when I am unhappy. (In other words: I can either live a drama or I can invent a drama—but I do not have the capacity to do both at the same time.)

Emotional pain makes me the opposite of a deep person;

it renders my life narrow and thin and isolated. My suffering takes this whole thrilling and gigantic universe and shrinks it down to the size of my own unhappy head. When my personal devils take over, I can feel my creative angels retreating. They watch my struggle from a safe distance, but they worry. Also, they grow impatient. It's almost as if they're saying, "Lady, please—hold it together! We've got so much more work to do!"

My desire to work—my desire to engage with my creativity as intimately and as freely as possible—is my strongest personal incentive to fight back against pain, by any means necessary, and to fashion a life for myself that is as sane and healthy and stable as it can possibly be.

But that's only because of what I have chosen to trust, which is quite simply: *love.*

Love over suffering, always.

Choose What to Trust

If you choose to go the other way, though (if you choose to trust suffering over love), be aware that you are building your house upon a battlefield. And when so many people treat their creative process as a war zone, is it any wonder there are such severe casualties? So much despair, so much darkness. And at such a cost!

I won't even attempt to list the names of all the writers, poets, artists, dancers, composers, actors, and musicians who have committed suicide in the past century, or who died long before their time from that slowest of suicidal tactics, alcoholism. (You want the numbers? The Internet will give you the numbers. But believe me, it's a grim reaping.) These lost prodigies were unhappy for an infinite variety of reasons, to be sure, though I'm willing to bet that they had all—at least for one flowering moment of their lives—once loved their work. Yet if you'd asked any of these gifted, troubled souls whether they'd ever believed that their work *loved them in return*, I suspect they would've said no.

But why wouldn't it have?

This is my question, and I think it's a fair one: Why would your creativity *not* love you? It came to you, didn't it? It drew itself near. It worked itself into you, asking for your attention and your devotion. It filled you with the desire to make and do interesting things. Creativity wanted a relationship with you. That must be for a reason, right? Do you honestly believe that creativity went through all the trouble of breaking into your consciousness only because it wanted to kill you?

That doesn't even make sense! How does creativity possibly benefit from such an arrangement? When Dylan Thomas dies, there are no more Dylan Thomas poems; that channel is silenced forever, terribly. I cannot imagine a universe in which creativity would possibly desire that outcome. I can only imagine that creativity would much prefer a world in which Dylan Thomas had continued to live and to produce, for a long natural life. Dylan Thomas and a thousand others, besides. There's a hole in our world from all the art those people did not make—there is a hole in *us* from the loss of their work—and I cannot imagine this was ever anyone's divine plan.

Because think about it: If the only thing an idea wants is to be made manifest, then why would that idea deliberately harm *you*, when you are the one who might be able to bring it forth? (Nature provides the seed; man provides the garden; each is grateful for the other's help.)

Is it possible, then, that creativity is not fucking with us at all, but that we have been fucking with it?

Stubborn Gladness

All I can tell you for certain is that my entire life has been shaped by an early decision to reject the cult of artistic martyrdom, and instead to place my trust in the crazy notion that *my work loves me as much as I love it*—that it wants to play with me as much as I want to play with it—and that this source of love and play is boundless.

I have chosen to believe that a desire to be creative was encoded into my DNA for reasons I will never know, and that creativity will not go away from me unless I forcibly kick it away, or poison it dead. Every molecule of my being has always pointed me toward this line of work—toward language, storytelling, research, narrative. If destiny didn't want me to be a writer, I figure, then it shouldn't have made me one. But it *did* make me one, and I've decided to meet that destiny with as much good cheer and as little drama as I can—because how I choose to handle myself as a writer is entirely my own choice. I can make my creativity into a killing field, or I can make it into a really interesting cabinet of curiosities.

I can even make it into an act of prayer.

My ultimate choice, then, is to always approach my work from a place of stubborn gladness.

I worked for years with stubborn gladness before I was published. I worked with stubborn gladness when I was still an unknown new writer, whose first book sold just a handful of copies—mostly to members of my own family. I worked with stubborn gladness when I was riding high on a giant best seller. I worked with stubborn gladness when I was not riding high on a giant best seller anymore, and when my subsequent books did not sell millions of copies. I worked with stubborn gladness when critics praised me, and I worked with stubborn gladness when critics made fun of me. I've held to my stubborn gladness when my work is going badly, and also when it's going well.

I don't ever choose to believe that I've been completely abandoned in the creative wilderness, or that there's reason for me to panic about my writing. I choose to trust that inspiration is always nearby, the whole time I'm working, trying its damnedest to impart assistance. It's just that inspiration comes from another world, you see, and it speaks a language entirely unlike my own, so sometimes we have trouble understanding each other. But inspiration is still sitting there right beside me, and it is *trying*. Inspiration is trying to send me messages in every form it can—through dreams, through portents, through clues, through coincidences, through déjà vu, through kismet, through surprising waves of attraction and reaction, through the chills that run up my arms, through the hair that stands up on the back of my neck, through the pleasure of something new and surprising, through stubborn ideas that keep me awake all night long . . . *whatever works.*

Inspiration is always trying to work with me.

So I sit there and I work, too.

That's the deal.

I trust it; it trusts me.

Choose Your Delusion

Is this delusional?

Is it delusional of me to place infinite trust in a force that I cannot see, touch, or prove—a force that might not even actually exist?

Okay, for the sake of argument, let's call it totally delusional.

But is it any more delusional than believing that only your suffering and your pain are authentic? Or that you are *alone*—that you have no relationship whatsoever with the universe that created you? Or that you have been singled out by destiny as specially cursed? Or that your talents were given to you for the mere purpose of destroying you?

What I'm saying is this: If you're going to live your life based on delusions (and you are, because we all do), then why not at least select a delusion that is helpful?

Allow me to suggest this one:

The work wants to be made, and it wants to be made through you.

The Martyr vs. the Trickster

But in order to let go of the addiction to creative suffering, you must reject the way of the martyr and embrace the way of the trickster.

We all have a bit of trickster in us, and we all have a bit of martyr in us (okay, some of us have a *lot* of martyr in us), but at some point in your creative journey you will have to make a decision about which camp you wish to belong to, and therefore which parts of yourself to nourish, cultivate, and bring into being. Choose carefully. As my friend the radio personality Caroline Casey always says: "Better a trickster than a martyr be."

What's the difference between a martyr and a trickster, you ask?

Here's a quick primer.

Martyr energy is dark, solemn, macho, hierarchical, fundamentalist, austere, unforgiving, and profoundly rigid.

Trickster energy is light, sly, transgender, transgressive, animist, seditious, primal, and endlessly shape-shifting.

Martyr says: "I will sacrifice everything to fight this unwinnable war, even if it means being crushed to death under a wheel of torment."

Trickster says: "Okay, you enjoy that! As for me, I'll be over here in this corner, running a successful little black market operation on the side of your unwinnable war."

Martyr says: "Life is pain."

Trickster says: "Life is interesting."

Martyr says: "The system is rigged against all that is good and sacred."

Trickster says: "There is no system, everything is good, and nothing is sacred."

Martyr says: "Nobody will ever understand me."

Trickster says: "Pick a card, any card!"

Martyr says: "The world can never be solved."

Trickster says: “Perhaps not . . . but it can be *gamed*.”

Martyr says: “Through my torment, the truth shall be revealed.”

Trickster says: “I didn’t come here to suffer, pal.”

Martyr says: “Death before dishonor!”

Trickster says: “Let’s make a deal.”

Martyr always ends up dead in a heap of broken glory, while Trickster trots off to enjoy another day.

Martyr = Sir Thomas More.

Trickster = Bugs Bunny.

Trickster Trust

I believe that the original human impulse for creativity was born out of pure trickster energy. Of course it was! Creativity wants to flip the mundane world upside down and turn it inside out, and that’s exactly what a trickster does best. But somewhere in the last few centuries, creativity got kidnapped by the martyrs, and it’s been held hostage in their camp of suffering ever since. I believe this turn of events has left art feeling very sad. It has definitely left a lot of artists feeling very sad.

It's time to give creativity back to the tricksters, is what I say.

The trickster is obviously a charming and subversive figure. But for me, the most wonderful thing about a good trickster is that he *trusts*. It may seem counterintuitive to suggest this, because he can seem so slippery and shady, but the trickster is full of trust. He trusts himself, obviously. He trusts his own cunning, his own right to be here, his own ability to land on his feet in any situation. To a certain extent, of course, he also trusts other people (in that he trusts them to be marks for his shrewdness). But mostly, the trickster trusts the universe. He trusts in its chaotic, lawless, ever-fascinating ways—and for this reason, he does not suffer from undue anxiety. He trusts that the universe is in constant play and, specifically, that it wants to play with *him*.

A good trickster knows that if he cheerfully tosses a ball out into the cosmos, that ball will be thrown back at him. It might be thrown back really hard, or it might be thrown back really crooked, or it might be thrown back in a cartoonish hail of missiles, or it might not be thrown back until the middle of next year—but that ball will eventually be thrown back. The trickster waits for the ball to return, catches it however it arrives, and then tosses it back out there into the void again, just to see what will happen. And he loves doing it, because the trickster (in all his cleverness) understands the one great cosmic truth that the martyr (in all his seriousness) can never grasp: *It's all just a game.*

A big, freaky, wonderful game.

Which is fine, because the trickster likes freaky.

Freaky is his natural environment.

The martyr hates freaky. The martyr wants to kill freaky. And in so doing, he all too often ends up killing himself.

A Good Trickster Move

I'm friends with Brené Brown, the author of *Daring Greatly* and other works on human vulnerability. Brené writes wonderful books, but they don't come easily for her. She sweats and struggles and suffers throughout the writing process, and always has. But recently, I introduced Brené to this idea that creativity is for tricksters, not for martyrs. It was an idea she'd never heard before. (As Brené explains: "Hey, I come from a background in academia, which is deeply entrenched in martyrdom. As in: 'You must labor and suffer for years in solitude to produce work that only four people will ever read.'")

But when Brené latched on to this idea of tricksterdom, she took a closer look at her own work habits and realized she'd been creating from far too dark and heavy a place within herself. She had already written several successful books, but all of them had been like a medieval road of trials for her—nothing but fear and anguish throughout the entire writing process. She'd never questioned any of this anguish, because she'd assumed it was all perfectly normal. After all, serious artists can only prove their merit through serious pain. Like so many creators before her, she had come to trust in that pain above all.

But when she tuned in to the possibility of writing from a place of trickster energy, she had a breakthrough. She realized that the act of writing itself was indeed genuinely difficult for her . . . but that *storytelling* was not. Brené is a captivating storyteller, and she loves public speaking. She's a fourth-generation Texan who can string a tale like nobody's business. She knew that when she spoke her ideas aloud, they flowed like a river. But when she tried to write those ideas down, they cramped up on her.

Then she figured out how to trick the process.

For her last book, Brené tried something new—a super-cunning trickster move of the highest order. She enlisted two trusted colleagues to join her at a beach house in Galveston to help her finish her book, which was under serious deadline.

She asked them to sit there on the couch and take detailed notes while she told them stories about the subject of her book. After each story, she would grab their notes, run into the other room, shut the door, and write down exactly what she had just told them, while they waited patiently in the living room. Thus, Brené was able to capture the natural tone of her own speaking voice on the page—much the way the poet Ruth Stone figured out how to capture poems as they moved through her. Then Brené would dash back into the living room and read aloud what she had just written. Her colleagues would help her to tease out the narrative even further, by asking her to explain herself with new anecdotes and stories, as again they took notes. And again Brené would grab those notes and go transcribe the stories.

By setting a trickster trap for her own storytelling, Brené figured out how to catch her own tiger by the tail.

Much laughter and absurdity were involved in this

process. They were, after all, just three girlfriends alone at a beach house. There were taco runs and visits to the Gulf. They had a blast. This scene is pretty much the exact opposite of the stereotypical image of the tormented artist sweating it out all alone in his garret studio, but as Brené told me, "I'm done with all that. Never again will I write about the subject of human connection while suffering in isolation." And her new trick worked like a charm. Never had Brené written faster, never had she written better, never had she written with such *trust*.

Mind you, this was not a book of comedy that she was writing, either. A lighthearted process does not necessarily need to result in a lighthearted product. Brené is a renowned sociologist who studies shame, after all. This was a book about vulnerability, failure, anxiety, despair, and hard-earned emotional resilience. Her book came out on the page just as deep and serious as it needed to be. It's just that she had a good time writing it, because she finally figured out how to game the system. In so doing, she finally accessed her own abundant source of Big Magic.

That's how a trickster gets the job done.

Lightly, lightly.

Ever lightly.

Lighten Up

The first short story I ever published was in 1993, in *Esquire* magazine. The story was called "Pilgrims." It was about a girl working on a ranch in Wyoming, and it was inspired by my own experience as a girl who had worked on a ranch in Wyoming. As usual, I sent the story out to a bunch of publications, unsolicited. As usual, everyone rejected it. Except one.

A young assistant editor at *Esquire* named Tony Freund plucked my story out of the slush pile and brought it to the editor in chief, a man named Terry McDonell. Tony suspected that his boss might like the story, because he knew Terry had always been fascinated with the American West. Terry did indeed like "Pilgrims," and he purchased it, and that's how I got my first break as a writer. It was the break of a lifetime. The story was slated to appear in the November issue of *Esquire*, with Michael Jordan on the cover.

A month before the issue was to go to press, however, Tony called me to say there was a problem. A major advertiser had pulled out, and as a result the magazine would need to be several pages shorter than planned that month. Sacrifices would have to be made; they were looking for volunteers. I was given a choice: I could either cut my story by 30 percent so that it would fit in the new, slimmer November issue, or I could pull it from the magazine entirely and hope it would find a home—intact—in some future issue.

"I can't tell you what to do," Tony said. "I will completely understand if you don't want to butcher your work like this. I think the story will indeed suffer from being amputated. It might be better for you, then, if we wait a few months and publish it intact. But I also have to warn you that the magazine world is an unpredictable business. There may be an argument for striking while the iron is hot. Your story might never get published if you hesitate now. Terry might lose interest in it or, who knows, he might even leave his job at *Esquire* and move to another magazine—and then your champion will be gone. So I don't know what to tell you. The choice is yours."

Do you have any idea what it means to cut 30 percent from a ten-page short story? I'd worked on that story for a year and a half. It was like polished granite by the time *Esquire* got their hands on it. There was not a superfluous word in it, I believed. What's more, I felt that "Pilgrims" was the best thing I'd ever written, and, as far as I knew, I might never write that well again. It was deeply precious to me, the blood of my blood. I couldn't imagine how the story would even make sense anymore, amputated like that. Above all, my dignity as an artist was offended by the very idea of mutilating my life's best work simply because a car company had pulled an advertisement from a men's magazine. What about integrity? What about honor? What about pride?

If artists do not uphold a standard of incorruptibility in this nefarious world, *who will*?

On the other hand, screw it.

Because let's be honest: It wasn't the Magna Carta we were talking about here; it was just a short story about a cowgirl and her boyfriend.

I grabbed a red pencil and I cut that thing down to the bone.

The initial devastation to the narrative was shocking. The story had no meaning or logic anymore. It was literary carnage—but that's when things started to get interesting. Looking over this hacked-up mess, it dawned upon me this was a rather fantastic creative challenge: Could I still manage to make it work? I began suturing the narrative back into a sort of sense. As I pieced and pinned sentences together, I realized that the cuts had indeed transformed the entire tone of the story, but not necessarily in a bad way. The new version was neither better nor worse than the old version; it was just profoundly different. It felt leaner and harder, not unappealingly austere.

I never would have written that way naturally—I hadn't known I *could* write that way—and that revelation alone intrigued me. (It was like one of those dreams where you discover a previously unknown room in your house, and you have that expansive feeling that your life has more possibility to it than you thought it did.) I was amazed to discover that my work could be played with so roughly—torn apart, chopped up, reassembled—and that it could still survive, perhaps even thrive, within its new parameters.

What you produce is not necessarily always sacred, I realized, just because you think it's sacred. What *is* sacred is the time that you spend working on the project, and what that time does to expand your imagination, and what that expanded imagination does to transform your life.

The more lightly you can pass that time, the brighter your existence becomes.

It Ain't Your Baby

When people talk about their creative work, they often call it their "baby"—which is the exact opposite of taking things lightly.

A friend of mine, a week before her new novel was to be

published, told me, "I feel like I'm putting my baby on the school bus for the first time, and I'm afraid the bullies will make fun of him." (Truman Capote stated it even more bluntly: "Finishing a book is just like you took a child out in the backyard and shot it.")

Guys, please don't mistake your creative work for a human child, okay?

This kind of thinking will only lead you to deep psychic pain. I'm dead serious about this. Because if you honestly believe that your work is your baby, then you will have trouble cutting away 30 percent of it someday—which you may very well need to do. You also won't be able to handle it if somebody criticizes or corrects your baby, or suggests that you might consider completely modifying your baby, or even tries to buy or sell your baby on the open market. You might not be able to release your work or share it at all—because how will that poor defenseless baby survive without you hovering over it and tending to it?

Your creative work is not your baby; if anything, you are *its* baby. Everything I have ever written has brought me into being. Every project has matured me in a different way. I am who I am today precisely because of what I have made and what it has made me into. Creativity has hand-raised me and forged me into an adult—starting with my experience with that short story "Pilgrims," which taught me how *not* to act like a baby.

All of which is to say that, yes, in the end, I did squeeze an abbreviated version of "Pilgrims" into the November 1993 issue of *Esquire* by the skin of its teeth. A few weeks later, as fate would have it, Terry McDonell (my champion) did indeed leave his job as editor in chief of the magazine. Whatever short stories and feature articles he left behind never saw the light of day. Mine would have been among them, buried in a shallow grave, had I not been willing to make those cuts.

But I did make the cuts, thank heavens, and the story was cool and different because of it—and I got my big break. My story caught the eye of the literary agent who signed me up, and who has now guided my career with grace and precision for more than twenty years.

When I look back on that incident, I shudder at what I almost lost. Had I been more prideful, somewhere in the world today (probably in the bottom of my desk drawer) there would be a short story called "Pilgrims," ten pages long, which nobody would've ever read. It would be untouched and pure, like polished granite, and I might still be a bartender.

I also think it's interesting that, once "Pilgrims" was published in *Esquire*, I never really thought about it again.

It was not the best thing I would ever write. Not even close. I had so much more work ahead of me, and I got busy with that work. "Pilgrims" was not a consecrated relic, after all. It was just a *thing*—a thing that I had made and loved, and then changed, and then remade, and still loved, and then published, and then put aside so that I could go on to make other things.

Thank God I didn't let it become my undoing. What a sad and self-destructive act of martyrdom that would have been, to have rendered my writing so inviolable that I defended its sanctity to its very death. Instead, I put my trust in play, in pliancy, in trickery. Because I was willing to be light with my work, that short story became not a grave, but a doorway that I stepped through into a wonderful and bigger new life.

Be careful of your dignity, is what I am saying.

It is not always your friend.

Passion vs. Curiosity

May I also urge you to forget about passion?

Perhaps you are surprised to hear this from me, but I am somewhat against passion. Or at least, I am against the *preaching* of passion. I don't believe in telling people,

"All you need to do is to follow your passion, and everything will be fine." I think this can be an unhelpful and even cruel suggestion at times.

First of all, it can be an unnecessary piece of advice, because if someone has a clear passion, odds are they're already following it and they don't need anyone to tell them to pursue it. (That's kind of the definition of a passion, after all: an interest that you chase obsessively, almost because you have no choice.) But a lot of people don't know exactly what their passion is, or they may have multiple passions, or they may be going through a midlife change of passion—all of which can leave them feeling confused and blocked and insecure.

If you don't have a clear passion and somebody blithely tells you to go follow your passion, I think you have the right to give that person the middle finger. Because that's like somebody telling you that all you need in order to lose weight is to be thin, or all you need in order to have a great sex life is to be multiorgasmic: *That doesn't help!*

I'm generally a pretty passionate person myself, but not every single day. Sometimes I have no idea where my passion has gone off to. I don't always feel actively inspired, nor do I always feel certain about what to do next.

But I don't sit around waiting for passion to strike me. I

keep working steadily, because I believe it is our privilege as humans to keep making things for as long as we live, and because I enjoy making things. Most of all, I keep working because I trust that creativity is always trying to find me, even when I have lost sight of it.

So how do you find the inspiration to work when your passion has flagged?

This is where curiosity comes in.

Devotion to Inquisitiveness

I believe that curiosity is the secret. Curiosity is the truth and the way of creative living. Curiosity is the alpha and the omega, the beginning and the end. Furthermore, curiosity is accessible to everyone. Passion can seem intimidatingly out of reach at times—a distant tower of flame, accessible only to geniuses and to those who are specially touched by God. But curiosity is a milder, quieter, more welcoming, and more democratic entity. The stakes of curiosity are also far lower than the stakes of passion. Passion makes you get divorced and sell all your possessions and shave your head and move to Nepal. Curiosity doesn't ask nearly so much of you.

In fact, curiosity only ever asks one simple question: "Is there *anything* you're interested in?"

Anything?

Even a tiny bit?

No matter how mundane or small?

The answer need not set your life on fire, or make you quit your job, or force you to change your religion, or send you into a fugue state; it just has to capture your attention for a moment. But in that moment, if you can pause and identify even *one tiny speck* of interest in something, then curiosity will ask you to turn your head a quarter of an inch and look at the thing a wee bit closer.

Do it.

It's a clue. It might seem like nothing, but it's a clue. Follow that clue. Trust it. See where curiosity will lead you next. Then follow the next clue, and the next, and the next. Remember, it doesn't have to be a voice in the desert; it's just a harmless little scavenger hunt. Following that scavenger hunt of curiosity can lead you to amazing, unexpected places. It may even eventually lead you to your passion—albeit through a strange, untraceable passageway of back alleys, underground caves, and secret doors.

Or it may lead you nowhere.

You might spend your whole life following your curiosity and have absolutely nothing to show for it at the end—except one thing. You will have the satisfaction of knowing that you passed your entire existence in devotion to the noble human virtue of inquisitiveness.

And that should be more than enough for anyone to say that they lived a rich and splendid life.

The Scavenger Hunt

Let me give you an example of where the scavenger hunt of curiosity can lead you.

I've already told you the story of the greatest novel I never wrote—that book about the Amazon jungle, which I neglected to nurture, and which eventually jumped out of my consciousness and into Ann Patchett's consciousness. *That* book had been a passion project. That idea had come to me in a brain wave of physical and emotional excitement and inspiration. But then I got distracted by life's exigencies, and I didn't work on that book, and it left me.

So it goes, and so it went.

After that Amazon jungle idea was gone, I didn't have

another brain wave of physical and emotional excitement and inspiration right away. I kept waiting for a big idea to arrive, and I kept announcing to the universe that I was ready for a big idea to arrive, but no big ideas arrived. There were no goose bumps, no hairs standing up on the back of my neck, no butterflies in my stomach. There was no miracle. It was like Saint Paul rode his horse all the way to Damascus and nothing happened, except maybe it rained a bit.

Most days, this is what life is like.

I poked about for a while in my everyday chores—writing e-mails, shopping for socks, resolving small emergencies, sending out birthday cards. I took care of the orderly business of life. As time ticked by and an impassioned idea still had not ignited me, I didn't panic. Instead, I did what I have done so many times before: I turned my attention away from passion and toward curiosity.

I asked myself, *Is there* anything *you're interested in right now, Liz?*

Anything?

Even a tiny bit?

No matter how mundane or small?

It turned out there was: gardening.

(I know, I know—contain your excitement, everyone! *Gardening!*)

I had recently moved to a small town in rural New Jersey. I'd bought an old house that came with a nice backyard. Now I wanted to plant a garden in that backyard.

This impulse surprised me. I'd grown up with a garden—a huge garden, which my mother had managed efficiently—but I'd never been much interested in it. As a lazy child, I'd worked quite hard *not* to learn anything about gardening, despite my mother's best efforts to teach me. I had never been a creature of the soil. I didn't love country life back when I was a kid (I found farm chores boring, difficult, and sticky) and I had never sought it out as an adult. An aversion to the hard work of country living is exactly why I'd gone off to live in New York City, and also why I'd become a traveler—because I didn't want to be any kind of farmer. But now I'd moved to a town even smaller than the town in which I'd grown up, and now I wanted a garden.

I didn't *desperately* want a garden, understand. I wasn't prepared to die for a garden, or anything. I just thought a garden would be nice.

Curious.

The whim was small enough that I could have ignored it. It barely had a pulse. But I didn't ignore it. Instead, I followed that small clue of curiosity and I planted some things.

As I did so, I realized that I knew more about this gardening business than I thought I knew. Apparently, I had accidentally learned some stuff from my mother back when I was a kid, despite my very best efforts not to. It was satisfying, to uncover this dormant knowledge. I planted some more things. I recalled some more childhood memories. I thought more about my mother, my grandmother, my long ancestry of women who worked the earth. It was nice.

As the season passed, I found myself seeing my backyard with different eyes. What I was raising no longer looked like my mother's garden; it was starting to look like my own garden. For instance, unlike my mom, a masterful vegetable gardener, I wasn't all that interested in vegetables. Rather, I longed for the brightest, showiest flowers I could get my hands on. Furthermore, I discovered that I didn't want to merely cultivate these plants; I also wanted to know stuff about them. Specifically, I wanted to know where they had come from.

Those heirloom irises that ornamented my yard, for instance—what was their origin? I did exactly one minute of research on the Internet and learned that my irises were not indigenous to New Jersey; they had, in fact, originated in Syria.

That was kind of cool to discover.

Then I did some more research. The lilacs that grew around my property were apparently descendants of similar bushes that had once bloomed in Turkey. My tulips also originated in Turkey—though there'd been a lot of interfering Dutchmen, it turned out, between those original wild Turkish tulips and my domesticated, fancy varieties. My dogwood was local. My forsythia wasn't, though; that came from Japan. My wisteria was also rather far from home; an English sea captain had brought the stuff over to Europe from China, and then British settlers had brought it to the New World—and rather recently, actually.

I started running background checks on every single plant in my garden. I took notes on what I was learning. My curiosity grew. What intrigued me, I realized, was not so much my garden itself, but the botanical history behind it—a wild and little-known tale of trade and adventure and global intrigue.

That could be a book, right?

Maybe?

I kept following the trail of curiosity. I elected to trust completely in my fascination. I elected to believe that I was interested in all this botanical trivia for a good reason. Accordingly, portents and coincidences began to appear before me, all related to this newfound interest in botanical history. I stumbled upon the right books, the right people, the right opportunities. For instance: The expert whose advice I needed to seek about the history of mosses lived—it turned out—only a few minutes from my grandfather's house in rural upstate New York. And a two-hundred-year-old book that I had inherited from my great-grandfather held the key I'd been searching for—a vivid historic character, worthy of embellishing into a novel.

It was all right in front of me.

Then I started to go a little crazy with it.

My search for more information about botanical exploration eventually led me around the planet—from my backyard in New Jersey to the horticultural libraries of England; from the horticultural libraries of England to the medieval pharmaceutical gardens of Holland; from the medieval pharmaceutical gardens of Holland to the moss-covered caves of French Polynesia.

Three years of research and travel and investigation later, I finally sat down to begin writing *The Signature of All Things*—a novel about a fictional family of nineteenth-century botanical explorers.

It was a novel I never saw coming. It had started with nearly *nothing*. I did not leap into that book with my hair on fire; I inched toward it, clue by clue. But by the time I looked up from my scavenger hunt and began to write, I was completely consumed with passion about nineteenth-century botanical exploration. Three years earlier, I had never even *heard* of nineteenth-century botanical exploration—all I'd wanted was a modest garden in my backyard!—but now I was writing a massive story about plants, and science, and evolution, and abolition, and love, and loss, and one woman's journey into intellectual transcendence.

So it worked. But it only worked because I said *yes* to every single tiny clue of curiosity that I had noticed around me.

That's Big Magic, too, you see.

It's Big Magic on a quieter scale, and on a slower scale, but make no mistake about it—it's still Big Magic.

You just have to learn how to trust it.

It's all about the *yes*.

That's Interesting

The creators who most inspire me, then, are not necessarily the most passionate, but the most curious.

Curiosity is what keeps you working steadily, while hotter emotions may come and go. I like that Joyce Carol Oates writes a new novel every three minutes—and on such a wide range of subjects—because so many things seem to fascinate her. I like that James Franco takes whatever acting job he wants (serious drama one minute, campy comedy the next) because he recognizes that it doesn't all have to earn him an Oscar nomination—and I like that, between acting gigs, he also pursues his interests in art, fashion, academia, and writing. (Is his extracurricular creativity any good? *I don't care!* I just like that the dude does whatever he wants.) I like that Bruce Springsteen doesn't merely create epic stadium anthems, but also once wrote an entire album based on a John Steinbeck novel. I like that Picasso messed around with ceramics.

I once heard the director Mike Nichols speak about his prolific film career, and he said that he'd always been really interested in his failures. Whenever he saw one of them airing on late-night TV, he would sit down and watch it all over again—something that he never did with his successes. He would watch with curiosity, thinking, *That's so interesting, how that scene didn't work out . . .*

No shame, no despair—just a sense that it's all very interesting. Like: Isn't it funny how sometimes things work and other times they don't? Sometimes I think that the difference between a tormented creative life and a tranquil creative life is nothing more than the difference between the word *awful* and the word *interesting*.

Interesting outcomes, after all, are just awful outcomes with the volume of drama turned way down.

I think a lot of people quit pursuing creative lives because they're scared of the word *interesting*. My favorite meditation teacher, Pema Chödrön, once said that the biggest problem she sees with people's meditation practice is that they quit just when things are starting to get interesting. Which is to say, they quit as soon as things aren't easy anymore, as soon as it gets painful, or boring, or agitating. They quit as soon as they see something in their minds that scares them or hurts them. So they miss the good part, the wild part, the transformative part—the part when you push past the difficulty and enter into some raw new unexplored universe within yourself.

And maybe it's like that with every important aspect of your life. Whatever it is you are pursuing, whatever it is you are seeking, whatever it is you are creating, be careful not to quit too soon. As my friend Pastor Rob Bell warns: "Don't rush through the experiences and circumstances that have the most capacity to transform you."

Don't let go of your courage the moment things stop being easy or rewarding.

Because that moment?

That's the moment when *interesting* begins.

Hungry Ghosts

You will fail.

It sucks, and I hate to say it, but it's true. You will take creative risks, and often they will not pan out. I once threw away an entire completed book because it didn't work. I diligently finished the thing, but it really didn't work, so I ended up throwing it away. (I don't know why it didn't work! How can I know? What am I, a book coroner? I have no certificate for the cause of death. *The thing just didn't work!*)

It makes me sad when I fail. It disappoints me. Disappointment can make me feel disgusted with myself, or surly toward others. By this point in my life, though, I've learned how to navigate my own disappointment without plummeting too far into death spirals of shame, rage, or inertia. That's because, by this point in my life, I have come to understand what part of me is suffering when I fail: It's just my ego.

It's that simple.

Now, I've got nothing against egos, broadly speaking. We all have one. (Some of us might even have *two*.) Just as you need your fear for basic human survival, you also need your ego to provide you with the fundamental outlines of selfhood—to help you proclaim your individuality, define your desires, understand your preferences, and defend your borders. Your ego, simply put, is what makes you who you are. Without one, you're nothing but an amorphous blob. Therefore, as the sociologist and author Martha Beck says of the ego, "Don't leave home without it."

But do not let your ego totally run the show, or it will shut down the show. Your ego is a wonderful servant, but it's a terrible master—because the only thing your ego ever wants is reward, reward, and more reward. And since there's never enough reward to satisfy, your ego will always be disappointed. Left unmanaged, that kind of disappointment will rot you from the inside out. An unchecked ego is what the Buddhists call "a hungry ghost"—forever famished, eternally howling with need and greed.

Some version of that hunger dwells within all of us. We all have that lunatic presence, living deep within our guts, that refuses to ever be satisfied with anything. I have it, you have it, we all have it. My saving grace is this, though: *I know that I am not only an ego; I am also a soul.* And I know that my soul doesn't care a whit about reward or failure. My soul is not guided by dreams of praise or fears of criticism. My soul doesn't even have language for such notions. My soul, when I tend to it, is a far more expansive and fascinating source of guidance than my ego will ever be, because my soul desires only one thing: *wonder.* And since creativity is my most efficient pathway to wonder, I take refuge there, and it feeds my soul, and it quiets the hungry ghost—thereby saving me from the most dangerous aspect of myself.

So whenever that brittle voice of dissatisfaction emerges within me, I can say, "Ah, my ego! There you are, old friend!" It's the same thing when I'm being criticized and I notice myself reacting with outrage, heartache, or defensiveness. It's just my ego, flaring up and testing its power. In such circumstances, I have learned to watch my heated emotions carefully, but I try not to take them too seriously, because I know that it's merely my ego that has been wounded—never my soul. It is merely my ego that wants revenge, or to win the biggest prize. It is merely my ego that wants to start a Twitter war against a hater, or to sulk at an insult, or to quit in righteous indignation because I didn't get the outcome I wanted.

At such times, I can always steady my life once more by returning to my soul. I ask it, "And what is it that *you* want, dear one?"

The answer is always the same: "More wonder, please."

As long as I'm still moving in that direction—toward wonder—then I know I will always be fine in my soul, which is where it counts. And since creativity is still the most effective way for me to access wonder, I choose *it.* I choose to block out all the external (and internal) noise and distractions, and to come home again and again to creativity. Because without that source of wonder, I know that I am doomed. Without it, I will forever wander the world in a state of bottomless dissatisfaction—nothing but a howling ghost, trapped in a body made of slowly deteriorating meat.

And that ain't gonna do it for me, I'm afraid.

Do Something Else

So how do you shake off failure and shame in order to keep living a creative life?

First of all, forgive yourself. If you made something and it didn't work out, let it go. Remember that you're nothing but a beginner—even if you've been working on your craft for fifty years. We are all just beginners here, and we shall all die beginners. So let it go. Forget about the last project, and go searching with an open heart for the next one. Back when I was a writer for *GQ* magazine, my editor in chief, Art Cooper, once read an article I'd been working on for five months (an in-depth travel story about Serbian politics that had cost the magazine a small fortune, by the way), and he came back to me an hour later with this response: "This is no good, and it will never be any good. You don't have the capacity to write this story, as it turns out. I don't want you to waste another minute on this thing. Move on to the next assignment immediately, please."

Which was rather shocking and abrupt, but, holy cow—talk about *efficiency*!

Dutifully, I moved on.

Next, next, next—always next.

Keep moving, keep going.

Whatever you do, try not to dwell too long on your failures. You don't need to conduct autopsies on your disasters. You don't need to know what anything means. Remember: The gods of creativity are not obliged to explain anything to us. Own your disappointment, acknowledge it for what it is, and move on. Chop up that failure and use it for bait to try to catch another project. Someday it might all make sense to you—why you needed to go through this botched-up mess in order to land in a better place. Or maybe it will never make sense.

So be it.

Move on, anyhow.

Whatever else happens, stay busy. (I always lean on this

wise advice, from the seventeenth-century English scholar Robert Burton, on how to survive melancholy: "Be not solitary, be not idle.") Find something to do—*anything*, even a different sort of creative work altogether—just to take your mind off your anxiety and pressure. Once, when I was struggling with a book, I signed up for a drawing class, just to open up some other kind of creative channel within my mind. I can't draw very well, but that didn't matter; the important thing was that I was staying in communication with artistry at some level. I was fiddling with my own dials, trying to reach inspiration in any way possible. Eventually, after enough drawing, the writing began to flow again.

Einstein called this tactic "combinatory play"—the act of opening up one mental channel by dabbling in another. This is why he would often play the violin when he was having difficulty solving a mathematical puzzle; after a few hours of sonatas, he could usually find the answer he needed.

Part of the trick of combinatory play, I think, is that it quiets your ego and your fears by lowering the stakes. I once had a friend who was a gifted baseball player as a young man, but he lost his nerve and his game fell apart. So he quit baseball and took up soccer for a year. He wasn't the greatest soccer player, but he liked it, and it didn't break his spirit so much when he failed, because his ego knew this truth: "Hey, I never claimed it was my game." What mattered is only that he was doing *something* physical, in order to bring himself back into his own skin, in order to get out of his own head, and in order to reclaim some sense of bodily ease. Anyhow, it was fun. After a year of kicking around a soccer ball for laughs, he went back to baseball, and suddenly he could play again—better and more lightly than ever.

In other words: If you can't do what you long to do, go do something else.

Go walk the dog, go pick up every bit of trash on the street outside your home, go walk the dog again, go bake a peach cobbler, go paint some pebbles with brightly colored nail polish and put them in a pile. You might think it's procrastination, but—with the right intention—it isn't; it's motion. And any motion whatsoever beats inertia, because inspiration will always be drawn to motion.

So wave your arms around. Make something. Do something. Do *anything.*

Call attention to yourself with some sort of creative action, and—most of all—*trust* that if you make enough of a glorious commotion, eventually inspiration will find its way home to you again.

Paint Your Bicycle

The Australian writer, poet, and critic Clive James has a perfect story about how once, during a particularly awful creative dry spell, he got tricked back to work.

After an enormous failure (a play that he wrote for the London stage, which not only bombed critically, but also ruined his family financially and cost him several dear friends), James fell into a dark morass of depression and shame. After the play closed, he did nothing but sit on the couch and stare at the wall, mortified and humiliated, while his wife somehow held the family together. He couldn't imagine how he would get up the courage to write anything else ever again.

After a long spell of this funk, however, James's young daughters finally interrupted his grieving process with a request for a mundane favor. They asked him if he would please do something to make their shabby old secondhand bicycles look a bit nicer. Dutifully (but not joyfully), James obeyed. He hauled himself up off the couch and took on the project.

First, he carefully painted the girls' bikes in vivid shades of red. Then he frosted the wheel spokes with silver and striped the seat posts to look like barbers' poles. But he didn't stop there. When the paint dried, he began to add hundreds of tiny silver and gold stars—a field of exquisitely detailed constellations—all over the bicycles. The girls grew impatient for him to finish, but James found that he simply could not stop painting stars ("four-pointed stars, six-pointed stars, and the very rare eight-pointed stars with peripheral dots"). It was incredibly satisfying work. When at last he was done, his daughters pedaled off on their magical new bikes, thrilled with the effect, while the great man sat there, wondering what on earth he was going to do with himself next.

The next day, his daughters brought home another little girl from the neighborhood, who asked if Mr. James might please paint stars on *her* bicycle, too. He did it. He trusted in the request. He followed the clue. When he was done, another child showed up, and another, and another. Soon there was a line of children, all waiting for their humble bicycles to be transformed into stellar objets d'art.

And so it came to pass that one of the most important writers of his generation spent several weeks sitting in his driveway, painting thousands and thousands of tiny stars on the bicycles of every child in the area. As he did so, he came to a slow discovery. He realized that "failure has a function. It asks you whether you really want to go on making things." To his surprise, James realized that the answer was *yes*. He really did want to go on making things. For the moment, all he wanted to make were beautiful stars on children's bicycles. But as he did so, something was healing within him. Something was coming back to life. Because when the last bike had been decorated, and every star in his personal cosmos had been diligently painted back into place, Clive James at last had this thought: *I will write about this one day.*

And in that moment, he was free.

The failure had departed; the creator had returned.

By doing something else—and by doing it with all his heart—he had tricked his way out of the hell of inertia and straight back into the Big Magic.

Fierce Trust

The final—and sometimes most difficult—act of creative trust is to put your work out there into the world once you have completed it.

The trust that I'm talking about here is the fiercest trust of all. This is not a trust that says "I am certain I will be a success"—because that is not fierce trust; that is innocent trust, and I am asking you to put aside your innocence for a moment and to step into something far more bracing and far more powerful. As I have said, and as we all know deep in our hearts, there is no guarantee of success in creative realms. Not for you, not for me, not for anyone. Not now, not ever.

Will you put forth your work anyhow?

I recently spoke to a woman who said, "I'm almost ready to start writing my book, but I'm having trouble trusting that the universe will grant me the outcome I want."

Well, what could I tell her? I hate to be a buzzkill, but the universe might *not* grant her the outcome she wants. Without a doubt, the universe will grant her some kind of outcome. Spiritually minded people would even argue that the universe will probably grant her the outcome she *needs*—but it might not grant her the outcome she *wants.*

Fierce trust demands that you put forth the work anyhow, because fierce trust knows that the outcome does not matter.

The outcome *cannot* matter.

Fierce trust asks you to stand strong within this truth: "You are worthy, dear one, regardless of the outcome. You will keep making your work, regardless of the outcome. You will keep sharing your work, regardless of the outcome.

You were born to create, regardless of the outcome. You will never lose trust in the creative process, even when you don't *understand* the outcome."

There is a famous question that shows up, it seems, in every single self-help book ever written: What would you do if you knew that you could not fail?

But I've always seen it differently. I think the fiercest question of all is this one: What would you do even if you knew that you might very well fail?

What do you love doing so much that the words *failure* and *success* essentially become irrelevant?

What do you love even more than you love your own ego?

How fierce is your trust in that love?

You might challenge this idea of fierce trust. You might buck against it. You might want to punch and kick at it. You might demand of it, "Why should I go through all the trouble to make something if the outcome might be *nothing*?"

The answer will usually come with a wicked trickster grin: "Because it's *fun*, isn't it?"

Anyhow, what else are you going to do with your time here on earth—*not* make things? Not do interesting stuff? Not follow your love and your curiosity?

There is always that alternative, after all. You have free will. If creative living becomes too difficult or too unrewarding for you, you can stop whenever you want.

But seriously: *Really?*

Because, think about it: *Then what?*

Walk Proudly

Twenty years ago, I was at a party, talking to a guy whose name I have long since forgotten, or maybe never even knew. Sometimes I think this man came into my life for the sole purpose of telling me this story, which has delighted and inspired me ever since.

The story this guy told me was about his younger brother, who was trying to be an artist. The guy was deeply admiring of his brother's efforts, and he told me an illustrative anecdote about how brave and creative and trusting his little brother was. For the purposes of this story, which I shall now recount here, let's call the little brother "Little Brother."

Little Brother, an aspiring painter, saved up all his money and went to France, to surround himself with beauty and inspiration. He lived on the cheap, painted every day, visited museums, traveled to picturesque locations, bravely spoke to everyone he met, and showed his work to anyone who would look at it. One afternoon, Little Brother struck up a conversation in a café with a group of charming young people, who turned out to be some species of fancy aristocrats. The charming young aristocrats took a liking to Little Brother and invited him to a party that weekend in a castle in the Loire Valley. They promised Little Brother that this was going to be the most fabulous party of the year. It would be attended by the rich, by the famous, and by several crowned heads of Europe. Best of all, it was to be a masquerade ball, where nobody skimped on the costumes. It was not to be missed. Dress up, they said, and join us!

Excited, Little Brother worked all week on a costume that he was certain would be a showstopper. He scoured Paris for materials and held back neither on the details nor the audacity of his creation. Then he rented a car and drove to the castle, three hours from Paris. He changed into his costume in the car and ascended the castle steps. He gave his name to the butler, who found him on the guest list and politely welcomed him in. Little Brother entered the ballroom, head held high.

Upon which he immediately realized his mistake.

This was indeed a costume party—his new friends had not misled him there—but he had missed one detail in translation: This was a *themed* costume party. The theme was "a medieval court."

And Little Brother was dressed as a lobster.

All around him, the wealthiest and most beautiful people of Europe were attired in gilded finery and elaborate period gowns, draped in heirloom jewels, sparkling with elegance as they waltzed to a fine orchestra. Little Brother, on the other hand, was wearing a red leotard, red tights, red ballet slippers, and giant red foam claws. Also, his face was painted red. This is the part of the story where I must tell you that Little Brother was over six feet tall and quite skinny—but with the long waving antennae on his head, he appeared even taller. He was also, of course, the only American in the room.

He stood at the top of the steps for one long, ghastly moment. He almost ran away in shame. Running away in shame seemed like the most dignified response to the situation. But he didn't run. Somehow, he found his resolve. He'd come this far, after all. He'd worked tremendously hard to make this costume, and he was proud of it. He took a deep breath and walked onto the dance floor.

He reported later that it was only his experience as an aspiring artist that gave him the courage and the license to be so vulnerable and absurd. Something in life had already taught him to just put it out there, whatever "it" is. That costume was what he had made, after all, so that's what he was bringing to the party. It was the best he had. It was *all* he had. So he decided to trust in himself, to trust in his costume, to trust in the circumstances.

As he moved into the crowd of aristocrats, a silence fell. The dancing stopped. The orchestra stuttered to a stop. The other guests gathered around Little Brother. Finally, someone asked him what on earth he was.

Little Brother bowed deeply and announced, "I am the court lobster."

Then: laughter.

Not ridicule—just joy. They loved him. They loved his sweetness, his weirdness, his giant red claws, his skinny ass in his bright spandex tights. He was the trickster among them, and so he made the party. Little Brother even ended up dancing that night with the Queen of Belgium.

This is how you must do it, people.

I have never created anything in my life that did not make me feel, at some point or another, like I was the guy who just walked into a fancy ball wearing a homemade lobster costume. But you must stubbornly walk into that room, regardless, and you must hold your head high. You made it; you get to put it out there. Never apologize for it, never explain it away, never be ashamed of it. You did your best with what you knew, and you worked with what you had, in the time that you were given. You were invited, and you showed up, and you simply cannot do more than that.

They might throw you out—but then again, they might not. They probably won't throw you out, actually. The ballroom is often more welcoming and supportive than you could ever imagine. Somebody might even think you're brilliant and marvelous. You might end up dancing with royalty.

Or you might just end up having to dance alone in the corner of the castle with your big, ungainly red foam claws waving in the empty air.

That's fine, too. Sometimes it's like that.

What you absolutely must *not* do is turn around and walk out. Otherwise, you will miss the party, and that would be a pity, because—please believe me—we did not come all this great distance, and make all this great effort, only to miss the party at the last moment.

Divinity

Accidental Grace

My final story comes from Bali—from a culture that does creativity quite differently than we do it here in the West. This story was told to me by my old friend and teacher Ketut Liyer, a medicine man who took me under his wing years ago, to share with me his considerable wisdom and grace.

As Ketut explained to me, Balinese dance is one of the world's great art forms. It is exquisite, intricate, and ancient. It is also holy. Dances are ritually performed in temples, as they have been for centuries, under the purview of priests. The choreography is vigilantly protected and passed from generation to generation. These dances are intended to do nothing less than to keep the universe intact. Nobody can claim that the Balinese do not take their dancing seriously.

Back in the early 1960s, mass tourism reached Bali for the first time. Visiting foreigners immediately became fascinated with the sacred dances. The Balinese are not shy about showing off their art, and they welcomed tourists to enter the temples and watch the dancing. They charged a small sum for this privilege, the tourists paid, and everyone was happy.

As touristic interest in this ancient art form increased, however, the temples became overcrowded with spectators. Things got a bit chaotic. Also, the temples were not particularly comfortable, as the tourists had to sit on the floor with the spiders and dampness and such. Then some bright Balinese soul had the terrific idea to bring the dancers to the tourists, instead of the other way around. Wouldn't it be nicer and more comfortable for the sunburned Australians if they could watch the dances from, say, a resort's swimming pool area, instead of from inside a damp, dark temple? Then the tourists could have a cocktail at the same time and really enjoy the entertainment! And the dancers could make more money, because there would be room for bigger audiences.

So the Balinese started performing their sacred dances at the resorts, in order to better accommodate the paying tourists, and everyone was happy.

Actually, not everyone was happy.

The more high-minded of the Western visitors were appalled. This was desecration of the sublime! These were sacred dances! This was *holy* art! You can't just do a sacred dance on the profane property of a beach resort—and for money, no less! It was an abomination! It was spiritual, artistic, and cultural prostitution! It was sacrilege!

These high-minded Westerners shared their concerns with the Balinese priests, who listened politely, despite the fact that the hard and unforgiving notion of "sacrilege" does not translate easily into Balinese thinking. Nor are the distinctions between "sacred" and "profane" quite so unambiguous as they are in the West. The Balinese priests were not entirely clear as to why the high-minded Westerners viewed the beach resorts as profane at all. (Did divinity not abide there, as well as anywhere else on earth?) Similarly, they were unclear as to why the friendly Australian tourists in their clammy bathing suits should not be allowed to watch sacred dances while drinking mai tais. (Were these nice-seeming and friendly people undeserving of witnessing beauty?)

But the high-minded Westerners were clearly upset by this whole turn of events, and the Balinese famously do not like to upset their visitors, so they set out to solve the problem.

The priests and the masters of the dance all got together

and came up with an inspired idea—an idea inspired by a marvelous ethic of lightness and trust. They decided that they would make up some new dances that were *not* sacred, and they would perform only these certified "divinity-free" dances for the tourists at the resorts. The sacred dances would be returned to the temples and would be reserved for religious ceremonies only.

And that is exactly what they did. They did it easily, too, with no drama and no trauma. Adapting gestures and steps from the old sacred dances, they devised what were essentially gibberish dances, and commenced performing these nonsense gyrations at the tourist resorts for money. And everyone was happy, because the dancers got to dance, the tourists got to be entertained, and the priests earned some money for the temples. Best of all, the high-minded Westerners could now relax, because the distinction between the sacred and the profane had been safely restored.

Everything was in its place—tidy and final.

Except that it was neither tidy nor final.

Because nothing is ever really tidy or final.

The thing is, over the next few years, those silly new meaningless dances became increasingly refined. The young boys and girls grew into them, and, working with a new sense of freedom and innovation, they gradually transformed the performances into something quite magnificent. In fact, the dances were becoming rather transcendent. In another example of an inadvertent séance, it appeared that those Balinese dancers—despite all their best efforts to be completely unspiritual—were unwittingly calling down Big Magic from the heavens, anyhow. Right there by the swimming pool. All they'd originally intended to do was entertain tourists and themselves, but now they were tripping over God every single night, and everyone could see it. It was arguable that the new dances had become even *more* transcendent than the stale old sacred ones.

The Balinese priests, noticing this phenomenon, had a wonderful idea: Why not borrow the new fake dances, bring them into the temples, incorporate them into the ancient religious ceremonies, and use them as a form of prayer?

In fact, why not *replace* some of those stale old sacred dances with these new fake dances?

So they did.

At which point the meaningless dances became holy dances, because the holy dances had become meaningless.

And everyone was happy—except for those high-minded Westerners, who were now thoroughly confused, because they couldn't tell anymore what was holy and what was profane. It had all bled together. The lines had blurred between high and low, between light and heavy, between right and wrong, between us and them, between God and earth . . . and the whole paradox was totally freaking them out.

Which I cannot help but imagine is what the trickster priests had in mind the entire time.

In Conclusion

Creativity is sacred, and it is not sacred.

What we make matters enormously, and it doesn't matter at all.

We toil alone, and we are accompanied by spirits.

We are terrified, and we are brave.

Art is a crushing chore and a wonderful privilege.

Only when we are at our most playful can divinity finally get serious with us.

Make space for all these paradoxes to be equally true inside your soul, and I promise—you can make anything.

So please calm down now and get back to work, okay?

The treasures that are hidden inside you are hoping you will say yes.

ACKNOWLEDGMENTS

I am deeply thankful to the following people for their assistance, their encouragement, and their inspiration: Katie Arnold-Ratliff, Brené Brown, Charles Buchan, Bill Burdin, Dave Cahill, Sarah Chalfant, Anne Connell, Trâm-Anh Doan, Markus Dohle, Rayya Elias, Miriam Feuerle, Brendan Fredericks, the late Jack Gilbert, Mamie Healey, Lydia Hirt, Eileen Kelly, Robin Wall Kimmerer, Susan Kittenplan, Geoffrey Kloske, Cree LeFavour, Catherine Lent, Jynne Martin, Sarah McGrath, Madeline McIntosh, Jose Nunes, Ann Patchett, Alexandra Pringle, Rebecca Saletan, Wade Schuman, Kate Stark, Mary Stone, Andrew Wylie, Helen Yentus—and, of course, the Gilberts and the Olsons, who taught me, by example, how to be a maker.

I am also grateful for the TED conference, for allowing me to stand upon their deeply serious stage (twice!) to speak of spiritual, whimsical, and creative matters. Those speeches led me to hone these thoughts, and I'm glad for it.

I thank Etsy for welcoming this project—and for giving a home to so many other creative projects, besides. You are everything I am talking about here.

Lastly, I send love and gratitude to my beautiful Facebook community. Without your questions, your thoughts, and your inspiring daily leaps of courageous self-expression, this book would not exist.

Before beginning the journey that led to the #1 *New York Times*–bestselling memoir *Eat Pray Love*, ELIZABETH GILBERT had already established herself as an award-winning writer of incomparable range, with a distinctly compelling voice—at times comic, often poignant, always inspiring. One of the most iconic and beloved writers of our time, Gilbert transcends genre. Each book she writes is an adventure into a vibrant, sensual, and unforgettable new world.

© Jennifer Schatten

PILGRIMS

Finalist for the PEN/Hemingway Award • A *New York Times* Notable Book

A story collection that announces Gilbert's compelling voice, her comic touch, and her rare sense of compassion.

Richly varied in setting and content, these short stories track diverse characters as they each pursue their own singular American pilgrimage. In the title story, a tough East Coast girl dares a Western cowboy to run off with her. In "The Famous Torn and Restored Cigarette Trick," a family of Hungarian musicians struggles for redemption in Pittsburgh, while in "At the Bronx Terminal Vegetable Market" an ignorant laborer is on an impossible and tragic quest for honor. "The heroes of *Pilgrims* . . . are everyday seekers" (*Harper's Bazaar*)—they may act blindly, especially about love, but they always act bravely, and they are unforgettable.

"Bizarre and fabulous . . . [Gilbert] moves stealthily, avoiding the temptation to grandstand, moralize, or, especially, patronize."

—The New York Times Book Review

T462-0115

STERN MEN

A wise and charming novel set off the coast of Maine.

Ruth Thomas is born into a feud fought for generations by two groups of local lobstermen over fishing rights for the waters that lie between their respective islands. At eighteen, she has returned from boarding school—smart as a whip, feisty, and irredeemably unromantic—determined to join the "stern men" and work the lobster boats. As the feud escalates, Ruth proves to be an unforgettable American heroine who is destined for greatness—and love—despite herself.

"Rich as drawn butter and as comical as the crawly crustacean itself . . . Gilbert has penned a Dickensian tale." —*USA Today*

T459-0115

EAT PRAY LOVE

One Woman's Search for Everything Across Italy, India and Indonesia

#1 *New York Times* bestseller

The book that touched the world and changed countless lives.

In her early thirties, Elizabeth Gilbert had everything a modern American woman was supposed to want—husband, country home, successful career—but instead of feeling happy and fulfilled, she was consumed by panic and confusion. This wise and rapturous book is the story of how she left behind all these outward marks of success, and of what she found in their place. Following a divorce and crushing depression, Gilbert set out to examine three different aspects of her nature, set against the backdrop of three different cultures: pleasure in Italy, devotion in India, and on the Indonesian island of Bali, a balance between worldly enjoyment and divine transcendence.

"Gilbert's prose is fueled by a mix of intelligence, wit, and colloquial exuberance that is close to irresistible."

—The New York Times Book Review

T458-0115

COMMITTED

A Love Story

#1 *New York Times* bestseller

An intimate and erudite celebration of love.

At the end of her memoir *Eat Pray Love*, Elizabeth Gilbert fell in love with Felipe, a Brazilian living in Indonesia. The couple swore eternal love, but also swore (as skittish divorce survivors) never to marry. However, providence intervened in the form of a U.S. government ultimatum: get married, or Felipe could never enter America again.

Told with Gilbert's trademark humor and intelligence, this fascinating meditation on compatibility and fidelity chronicles Gilbert's complex and sometimes frightening journey into second marriage, and will enthrall the millions of readers who made *Eat Pray Love* a number-one bestseller.

"Entertaining and illuminating."

—Curtis Sittenfeld, *The New York Times Book Review*

T460-0115

THE SIGNATURE OF ALL THINGS

A Novel

A *New York Times* bestseller

Named a Best Book of the Year by *The New York Times*, *O: The Oprah Magazine*, *The Washington Post*, the *Chicago Tribune*, and *The New Yorker*.

A glorious, sweeping novel of desire, ambition, and the thirst for knowledge.

Love, adventure, and discovery are at the heart of *The Signature of All Things*, which soars across the globe from America to Tahiti to tell the story of a brilliant woman named Alma Whittaker. Born in 1800 as the daughter of a charismatic botanical explorer, Alma quickly comes into her own within the world of plants and science. But as her research takes her deeper into the mysteries of evolution, she falls in love with a man who draws her in the opposite direction—into the realm of the spiritual, the divine, and the magical.

Written in the bold, questing spirit of the nineteenth century, Gilbert's spellbinding tale takes the reader to unexpected places as it tells of a remarkable woman with an unquenchable sense of wonder.

"Sumptuous . . . Gilbert's prose is by turns flinty, funny, and incandescent."
—***The New Yorker***

T457-0115

We invite you to join Liz on her socials:

GilbertLiz

GilbertLiz

Elizabeth_Gilbert_Writer

lizgilbertpins

Sign up for "Liz News," Liz's official newsletter, on her website: elizabethgilbert.com/liznews/

T463-0115